DON'T BUY A DUCK

STOP WASTING MONEY & ONLY
DO MARKETING THAT WORKS!

derek champagne

ISBN Hardcover: 978-0-692-62089-2
ISBN Paperback: 978-0-692-84278-2
ISBN eBook: 978-0-692-62088-5

Library of Congress Control Number: 2016900563

Printed in the United States of America

Research Coordinator: Valerie Champagne
Cover Illustration and Design: Logan Rhea
Interior Design: Ghislain Viau

To my amazing partner in life, Valerie, for turning my energy kinetic. To Emily and Eli for reminding me to appreciate the small (but significant) things and for keeping me young at heart.

Contents

CHAPTER ONE

Tired of Wasting Money on Marketing?

H ave you ever bought a duck? I have.

I mean that in both literal and metaphorical terms, but I know you're curious, so I'll start with the former and then we can talk about the latter.

I remember when I was growing up, it seemed that every car my parents owned had a special radar for yard sales, and a special braking feature for when my mother found one. During the time of my duck acquisition, it was a 1981 Oldsmobile station wagon: classic yard sale chariot. I was 8 years old, and my mom had given my brother and me $5 each to spend on the object of our choosing.

With all the sense of an 8-year-old, I chose a duck. He had a little string tied to his webbed foot advertising his price at $10;

he was perfect, I had to have him. I convinced my brother to go in on the duck with me, and I told my mom about my decision. "That's a duck," she said.

Obviously it was a duck. I nodded. He quacked.

"Are you sure you want to spend *all* your money on that?" She seemed to know something I didn't, but there was no talking me out of it.

"I have to have him." It absolutely, 100%, felt like the right thing to do in the moment.

There was no turning back. I paid for the duck and watched as he was gingerly placed into a cardboard box, which I carried into the car and into the backseat with my brother and me, and we took off for home. The buyer's remorse hit me a few minutes later as the duck popped out of the box, flying and squawking around the back of the car. That cute little duck I just *had to have* had morphed into a monstrous albatross, and it was on the attack.

Luckily, we were able to pull over and let him out into a neighbor's pond, where he looked right at home. I dubbed him Quackers before we pulled away and watched him swim happily about in the place where he would live out the rest of his natural days just as a duck should. I felt so relieved that the disaster seemed to be reversed; I wasn't going to be stuck with this wild animal I'd bought on impulse. But that sinking feeling of having wasted all of my money on a whim stuck with me.

In your life as a consumer, you've probably had this feeling. If you bought an actual duck like I did, then you definitely had this feeling. But even if your impulse buy was a big flat-screen TV, a designer dress that cost you more than your mortgage payment for that month, a new car, whatever it was, you can undoubtedly relate to the little pit in your stomach that starts to open up when you realize you've spent your money less than wisely.

And what about your professional life? Everyone from small business owners to C-level executives of major corporations has to struggle with purchase decisions. There's a great deal of pressure involved in making these decisions, especially if you're a small business owner, and many of your own personal assets (not to mention your time and energy) are tied up in your business. This is particularly true if, like many small business owners, you're looking to hand down what you've built to the future generations.

Particularly when it comes to decisions about marketing, the pressure has only ratcheted up over recent years as we're faced with more choices to make than ever before. Social media, digital media, viral video, grassroots marketing, traditional media, streaming services…the options and possibilities can start to feel as overwhelming as they are exciting. Marketing managers and small- to medium-size business owners are finding that in order to stand out, they're engaging in a dangerous game of guesswork. Not wanting to be left out in the cold, they'll bank all their marketing dollars on the next hot marketing tactic, only to find that they've bought a duck.

If this sounds familiar to you, you shouldn't despair. We've all been there; I can practically hear the sounds of those beating wings flapping against my head as Quackers crashed around the station wagon. The key to moving forward and growing—to avoiding the ducks—is to learn to recognize them and act strategically, propelling your business ahead with more than a gut feeling or an impulse.

That's where this book comes in. I've dedicated my career—my life's work—to helping clients avoid those crisis points and stumbling blocks that we've all fallen victim to at one time or another. I've managed marketing and branding for businesses across the country, including startups, banks, medical and dental offices, restaurants, automotive, IT, service sector, even an Ivy League university. And I've learned that ducks can come in all shapes and sizes, and out in the business world they can do a lot more damage than little Quackers did. I've seen a law firm entirely exhaust its *annual marketing budget* on billboards in only one county, getting no response from a contract they were locked into for a year. I've talked with a successful business owner who invested all of his money in a Search Engine Optimization (SEO) vendor who promised dramatic results, only to deliver next to nothing in return.

These lessons aren't pretty, but they are important. They are also not predictions; your future isn't set in stone, and you don't have to fall into these traps. My hope for you is that I'll be able to share some of my experiences with you so that you can learn from these mistakes—and successes—just like I learned a very valuable lesson that day in my mom's station wagon. So I'd like to start this journey with an arrangement, a challenge: I'll do my best to shine a light on both the pitfalls and the path around them, if you don't spend another penny in advertising until you've read this book.

And no matter what, please, I'm begging you: don't buy a duck!

* * *

Marketing matters. Your decisions about how to market matter, too. For some reason, though, and maybe it's simply a by-product of the complexity of the world today, businesses often seem to leave marketing up to chance and guesswork.

I don't think I'm out of line to say that you would never leave something like product manufacturing up to guesswork. You'd never put a product out there and hope it didn't fall to pieces once your customer took it out of the box or, heaven forbid, out on the road. So why is marketing any different?

It's not! I've been in a position to find that out the hard way, and I've been in a position to put my experience to work to shape and drive marketing strategy; I can tell you with certainty that strategy is the way to go. There are so many questions that businesses must ask when building a marketing strategy. How do you know if you're choosing the right venue for your message? Should you go with something like the Yellow Pages or something fresher, like Yelp? What will give you the best bang for your buck? Is your message reaching the right audience? Are you measuring the impact of your message, tracking and comparing it across outlets?

Even though these questions are just the tip of the iceberg, the view from up here can easily still seem dizzying. This is where getting perspective helps; with a systematic approach, even the most complicated problems can be compartmentalized into solvable bits. (I know it's hard to hear that when there's a duck flapping around in your car—or your office—but fear not, it's absolutely true.)

Oftentimes, I hear from clients that something's not working, that the billboards they bet the farm on brought in no business, or that direct mail is dead. It would be easy, particularly when you've got a business to run, to throw up your hands and stick your head in the sand. Or, if you can afford it, to spend more money trying to solve the problem, although that's what we call throwing good money after bad.

When I hear that something doesn't work, my first response is to go into what I call "audit mode" right away. I want to know *why* it doesn't work; it's not enough to just declare that something doesn't. When you start breaking down the data, you can isolate the problem area: Perhaps the message wasn't right. Perhaps the identity of the brand was confusing. It's entirely possible that the Yellow Pages are dead for your brand, yes, but what I'm saying is that you need to *look deeper*. It's through this deeper understanding that you can avoid buying a duck, or worse—a couple ducks.

Attaining this deeper understanding and gaining perspective requires the willingness to press pause on your spending (remember the challenge I presented earlier in the chapter?). It requires the willingness to work through message, identity, and other footwork before you get the gears turning on your advertising spending. I've also encountered clients with the opposite problem; frozen by fear of failure, and unsure of which way to turn their focus, they avoid pulling the trigger on advertising purchases. Maybe they've been burned in the past, or maybe they're confused about where to start.

This happens equally to startup companies as it does to organizations with multi-million-dollar budgets. If you find yourself in either of these situations, you absolutely shouldn't feel like you're out of your depth. But I *do* want you to feel like there's work to be done, and I want us to work through it together.

For every person or company that has bought a duck in the past, I've got more stories of success. I point to clients like Dr. Jordan Cooper, a successful business owner and best-selling author (www.ChasingtheBlueMarlin.com) with eight thriving dental practices (and growing) across his home state. From day one of becoming a business owner, Dr. Cooper knew he wanted to avoid getting stuck with a duck. He hired my firm to help him set up marketing campaigns correctly from the start, and to get a handle on marketing without falling victim to the paralyzing stress it seems to cause non-marketers. His business footprint continues growing year by year, no ducks in sight.

Or I point to clients like the $100-million parent brand that came to our agency when it sought to set up a new business in the service industry and needed to achieve market penetration quickly. We shepherded them from infancy through execution, able to set up their brand, messaging, plan, venues, execution strategy—all before going public. Making sure the tenets of a branding and advertising strategy are in place *before* a product goes to market is part of how companies set themselves up for success, rather than having to run a race starting from way behind the starting blocks.

Moving forward with systematic growth governed by time-tested principles is always, always, *always* preferable to playing catch-up. Too often, when companies find themselves stuck with a duck, they scramble and waste time, money, and energy with what I call "Band-Aid" marketing, or "blindfold" marketing. It's very much just what it sounds like—trying to fix an already festering wound, or moving blindly forward, throwing things out there with no rhyme or reason, hoping something sticks. Instead, there should always be a methodology for growth.

My aim in writing this book is to help you take the guess-work out of that methodology. I'll use examples from real-world companies—both startups and gold standards—to provide context and templates for marketing success. Taking the mystery out of marketing, revealing the man behind the curtain, however you want to put it—I want to make you more confident, more able to move forward, and more certain that you're going to be doing the right thing. I'm not foolish enough to suggest that everything can be solved with a formula, but what I can provide is a flexible framework that can be tailored to the needs of businesses large and small. You'll come away with a clear idea of what the best steps are, in what order those steps should be taken, where to spend your money, and how you should represent your brand to stand out from the competition. When we're finished, I want to be able to say that I've helped you build a plan for not only the *ethos* of your marketing, but its *execution* as well.

Finally, at the bottom of whatever trepidation, whatever questions, you might have about marketing, I hope that you can tap into a sense of excitement about the prospects in front of us, too. I'm a business owner, just like you; I go through my periods of doubt and worry all the time. I know that, particularly in this economy, particularly for smaller businesses, there's not a big margin of error—getting locked into an ugly duckling advertising contract (like the previous example of the billboards, or the Yellow Pages, or insert your own personal horror story here) can mean having to tighten your belt in other areas; that hurts, I know.

But I also know that marketing is *exciting*. Building an awareness of your brand or your product—whatever you've dedicated your professional and sometimes, particularly for you entrepreneurs, your personal life to—is *thrilling*. We're living in an era of unprecedented technological development, of an explosion of choice. We've been told that traditional advertising is dead, and that you have to get on board with the new mediums or you're going to get left behind. I have another challenge for you. Instead of thinking of that as a *bad* thing, think of it as a *good* thing. Think

of opportunities for growth, for change. Think about maximizing your resources, executing with purpose, and seeing real results. Think about what you'll be free to do once you've set yourself up for success—the people you'll be able to reach, the revenue you'll be able to gain, the confidence you'll have that your marketing is on the right track. That sounds pretty good, doesn't it?

See? Now we're talking.

Are you ready to set yourself up for success?

You've already taken the first step (reading this book!)—your next step is to receive a special invitation to our Business Leadership Series.

Visit: www.dontbuyaduck.com/bonus or text DUCK to 58885.

CHAPTER TWO

The Identity Crisis—A Brand's Bermuda Triangle

There's something to be said for the diamond in the rough. We all can think of one; that little hole-in-the-wall Mexican place that has the best tacos in town, the unassuming local coffee shop that serves the most out-of-this-world pastry this side of Paris. It's fun to find those places, and part of their charm is that their amazing offerings are secret. We know something most other people don't (and we don't have to deal with lines out the door to get what we want there.)

But when it comes to working with brands — be they multi-million-dollar giants or small startups — this kind of narrative is exactly what I *don't* like to hear. If I have a client with a stellar story and a product to match, I want *everyone* to know about it. I

want to hear people shouting from the rooftops from miles away. I want, and my client wants, the recognition that having a top-notch brand should bring.

I remember one day receiving a phone call from a potential client, a referral from an existing business contact. He had an interesting product — a stunt and private charter pilot who had an extensive collection of old airplanes, he wanted sponsors for a stunt show to be incorporated into airshows nationwide. But immediately being in audit mode, I felt a little confused by his pitch. When he told me that he'd been recently turned down by the History Channel, I asked to see what materials he had submitted to the network. I had to cringe a little bit when I opened the file: it was a Word document with a black-and-white photo of a WWII Wildcat fighter plane and a few logos of potential sponsors splashed across the page with some seemingly outrageous dollar figures.

I like a good underdog, though, and so I went to the gentleman's office to talk things out face to face. The "office," it turned out, was a large metal building comprising two oversized airplane hangars containing nearly a dozen airplanes and jets from his private collection. The centerpiece was a gleaming, lovingly restored WWII Wildcat fighter jet — the photo hadn't done it justice *at all* — one of the last 12 remaining operational in the world today. He excitedly told me he was in negotiations to purchase another from a museum.

Here was a successful businessperson with an amazing product and an amazing story, but he didn't know where to start in effectively telling the story of his brand. I'm forever thankful that I gave him a second chance; I was able to help him develop a professional brand, logos, website, sharp sponsorship materials, and an action

video that blew the Word document out of the water. And I'm able to point to his story as a clear example of the four crisis points in marketing that lead even great brands to get stuck: lack of identity, lack of message strategy, lack of or improper marketing tools, and lack of an organized plan or campaign. Over the last several years, I've isolated these commonly overlooked areas as pain points that cause marketing or advertising to falter.

If something resonates with you from the story above, I don't want you to be worried. I preach preventative medicine, and tackling these issues before you open your business or launch your brand can save years of frustration, money, and guesswork, not to mention time. But if you've already launched and found yourself stuck in a similar quagmire, that doesn't mean it's too late. In fact, I couldn't be more sympathetic to business owners who have these issues. There's just so much going on today, it can be incredibly hard to get a handle on how, when, and to whom to tell your story. Just look at the media landscape! In 1960, there were five marketing channels. Today? More than 70.[1]

With all of these options, it's even more crucial to address these different crisis points before you start navigating the waters out there. In this chapter, we'll tackle the first point—identity, both of your brand and of your target customer—in detail.

Who Are You?

Does your brand have a clear identity? Take Starbucks, for instance. When you drive by a Starbucks, you know exactly what

---

[1] Pardot B2B Marketing automation by SalesForce, http://www.slideshare.net/pardot/sshare-2013-demand-report

it would feel like to be sitting inside. When you see a Starbucks commercial, you can taste the deep vanilla flavor of your favorite latte. You can express what Starbucks stands for—the *experience* of drinking coffee there, reading the paper, and nibbling on a cookie.

What about your brand? If you were pressed to give an elevator pitch to an investor or a future customer about who you were — that is, given a very limited amount of time while you're stuck in the same small space — would you be able to do it? Having a clear handle on your identity as a brand is the first step to building and implementing a successful marketing strategy.

Years ago, I worked with a client with a thriving high-end practice. Operating during a time when the economy wasn't doing so hot, this doctor didn't want to accept insurance because it limited the type of treatment he wanted to offer. He had cultivated a client base that included patients who were concerned about their health and could afford to pay for top-notch procedures at out-of-pocket prices even in the depths of the Great Recession in 2008. It was an enviable position. But there was some confusion surrounding his branding and his message. He had a clear idea of who he wanted to be — a high-end specialist serving cash-only patients for complicated restorative procedures — but he wasn't sure how to articulate that in a way that would best reach his ideal target patient. His branding and materials didn't match what he offered; there was not a clear representation of the caliber of service he provided, and he wasn't communicating clearly to his potential clients. Simply put: he was attracting customers from a much poorer demographic and missing the top echelons that he wanted to serve.

The need for a clear story should obviously be addressed in any branded materials you have, but it should originate from the very core of your company. I'm fond of quoting a maxim from Jay Conrad Levinson, the father of guerilla marketing: "Marketing is every bit of contact your company has with anyone in the outside world. It has a beginning and a middle, but not an ending." This wonderful advice is applicable to so many points on the path to become a successful brand, but I'm leaning on it here to emphasize the fact that marketing isn't something that you can just start and stop. Marketing is everything, branding is everything; it's your identity, it's at the center of every interaction, no matter how large or small. (And it can be small—*Just Do It*, one of the most iconic slogans of our times, is three simple words!) It can be as small as the script your customer service person uses to answer the phone for a general question, or it can be as big and immediate as your logo or brand name.

If the name of your company is completely inscrutable—I once worked with a growing corporation in the service industry whose name was Amgine, or "enigma" spelled backward, and initially I couldn't for the life of me figure out what it was that they offered based on that name—a customer won't always stick around as long as I did to sort that out. So we went to the core of what they offered—weatherproofing technology for homes—and renamed them Weather Proofing Experts (www. WeatherProofingExperts.com). It made them easier to turn up in search engine results; it could be parsed out within a few seconds of conversation. It was clear.

We took it a step further for the brand, too, making sure that their new logo was just as easy to understand. The previous logo—a puzzle piece—was a clever nod to the old name, a reference to the "enigma." We kept the puzzle pieces in the new logo—it was clearly important to the company—but instead, the puzzle pieces became an umbrella that was sitting on top of a house. Looking at the logo, you could easily tell that this was a company that could protect your home from leaks and bad weather—at a glance. No games, no tricks to figure out.

I always tell clients that they should work to stay top of mind, tip of tongue. The ultimate goal is to make sure that long after your customers have encountered any of your marketing, they'll still be able to recall your service when they need it. When you've got a clear, consistent message, it makes your brand more shareable, giving it more value. Consider Apple—how you can tell if you're using an Apple product just by holding it in your hand, or that feeling you get when you unwrap a brand-new piece of Apple technology and see how sleek, simple, and pristine it looks. You can tell you're watching an Apple commercial even if you come in at the end of it. When you get to that point, you won't need sophisticated or complicated messaging to make yourself known—instead, you'll be a household name. Everyone from the top of your organization on down to your employees and then your customers themselves can clearly articulate that identity, magnifying your story through a powerful chamber of echoes.

If you've bothered to invest money in communicating with your customers, bottom line, you need to know who you are, and you need to use your story to make an emotional connection with their needs. Even the most intelligent and seasoned executives can become distracted by what they feel is clever or catchy, when the real thing to focus on is what sets them apart and why customers should connect with their brand. The end-user must always be kept in mind—they're paying the bills, after all.

It can be challenging to verbalize what we see in the mirror every day. I've fallen victim to this myself; it took my company a few rounds of exercises to finally distill ourselves down to the three things that we do well and find a way to share those three things in one sentence. It will take a little work to parse out how and what you need to be telling your customers, even when it comes from your most authentic selling proposition. But this part of the equation is pretty fun, when you get down to it. In figuring out who you are, what your brand offers, and what you want to communicate to your customers, you really get to write your story from the very first word on. You can start this process by asking yourself a few key questions:

- What is it that you do well?
- What do you want to be known for?
- What core services do you offer?
- What moods and emotions do you want customers to associate with your business? (For instance, do you want a "warm, friendly" brand?)

These are just a few of the questions you'll need to answer throughout the process, but I want you to start thinking about building your identity without getting too overwhelmed. I hope, instead, that you're getting excited. As marketing professionals, it's our duty and privilege to be a part of shaping the perception of a brand, long before a consumer has had any interaction with it. By teasing out what your core services and traits are and communicating those through everything you do, you're really setting the tone for what your future customers can expect from you.

Who Are Your Customers?

The second pain point that comes up for businesses is often that they don't have a clear idea of the identity of their target customer. As much as it's crucial to know who your company is, you must equally understand your customer. Another example from the dental world comes to mind here—and I like to point to my past experience consulting for dental practices for many reasons, but particularly because it can be tempting to lump customers into an overly simplistic identity. Yes, they all need dental care. Yes, they are all people with teeth! But no one, not even a medical or dental practice, is immune to needing to understand their niche. And no one, not even a medical or dental practice, is guaranteed a steady flow of customers without putting any work into it. In fact, in such a heavily populated market, it's even tougher to stand out—the more that businesses are raising their voices trying to explain what makes them stand out, the higher the stakes are for the brand that wants to truly cut through the clutter.

I had a client who was trying to stand out in a marketplace saturated with 48 dental providers in one geographic region. My client was booking at 90% with 25 years of experience, a rock star in her business. And yet, she still wasn't really standing out enough with an attribute that she could advertise that would truly make her unique, truly stand out from the competitors. I felt she had an outstanding service to provide, and I wanted to help her reach her full, unique branding potential by pulling away from the pack. So the first thing to take care of was obviously running an audit of what made her practice unique—addressing that first crisis point ("who are you?"). It quickly became clear that her office had a definite "Zen" vibe to it: there were water fountains, calming colors, meditative music in the air. The dentist herself was into the concept and had imparted that tranquility into her office. Coining the term "Zentistry," we proceeded with an ad campaign that truly was unique. No one else in the market had taken this approach, so this made her stand out.

But it wasn't enough to stop at the first crisis point. Once we'd been able to articulate her identity, we needed to go forward and really lock in on what her client base should be. Like the provider I mentioned earlier in the chapter, she served higher-end clients. Many of them had a bad experience with dentistry in the past, and found the Zen-like calm of her office to be soothing. Once she understood who these clients were, she could think about how best to reach them. She could reverse-engineer a marketing strategy by looking at what avenues would help her reach these particular clients and these particular clients alone. Instead of calling out with a general "Visit us for a warm, inviting, experience," she could combine these qualities with a crystal clear marker—Zentistry—that was hers and hers alone.

To help isolate the values that will enable you to break through the clutter and communicate clearly with your target in a language that resonates with them and motivates them to respond, you must truly look at your product through your customers' eyes. *Why* does your product matter to them? *Why* do they want it? *What need* does it satisfy for them? Yes, you need to educate them on the features that differentiate you from your competition. Yes, you need to get them acquainted with the history of your brand, its legacy, and its pedigree. But most important, you need to have a solid understanding of what matters to your client base so that you can then tailor your communication to addressing those needs.

This process is essential to devising a strategy for segmentation of your message, too. I've never come across a truly one-size-fits-all message, and it's important to identify if you can segment campaigns to directly address different niches of your customer base. This is where the proliferation of channels will come in handy—you won't have to rely on a megaphone to reach everyone in a given area when smaller, more targeted efforts on different platforms will do. As a bonus, it's much easier to make a true emotional connection when you're using a segmented approach, too; there's a certain lack of dissonance that you can always count on when you're talking directly to a consumer and directly addressing his or her needs with a product or brand.

Would you like additional tips & tools that will help you refine and polish your brand's story? We'd love to send the best and most up-to-date marketing trends directly to your inbox.

Visit: www.dontbuyaduck.com/bonus or text DUCK to 58885.

CHAPTER THREE

Why Brands Get Stuck: Other Crisis Points in Marketing

Identity—both of the brand and of its customers—is only the tip of the iceberg. Remember Levinson's admonition: "Marketing is every bit of contact your company has with anyone in the outside world." You must absolutely understand your identity and the identity of your target market in order to build a strong brand, but you can't stop there. Marketers also often stumble over these three areas, which overlap with identity but are part of larger structures that need to be sound in their own right: lack of message strategy, lack of or improper marketing tools, and lack of an organized plan or campaign.

What's Your Message?

Once you've done the important work of isolating the identity of both your company and your customers, the work must then be done to determine how you want your brand to be perceived. Your corporate identity, both internally and externally, must be brought into total alignment with this message. Your materials must communicate on an appropriate level with your client base— if you're a high-end jeweler, for instance, you don't want your materials to look like they were run off an in-house copy machine. Everything must have a similar look and feel; your presentation must be cohesive.

This doesn't mean that you won't have different targets; we'll talk a little more about the specific execution across programs later on in the book. I don't mean to say that you'll be running the same campaign on Facebook that you'll be running in print, for instance. But all of your messaging should have a sort of filter applied—not a stifling corporate overtone, but rather a unifying identity, a singular message. That Facebook campaign and print campaign, while taking place on two different platforms, should both be easily identifiable as belonging to your company. If you've done the work of isolating your identity as well as your customers' identity, this should follow pretty seamlessly.

If you were to lay all of your materials out on a table, what would that look like? Would they have a similar look and feel, or would they look like they were culled from two or three different agencies or brands? Even if the materials are meant for different audiences or different platforms, do they appear to work in concert or are they disjointed? Spending to operate one campaign is high-stakes enough—imagine how hard it is for a small business to effectively juggle three disjointed marketing campaigns at the same time! At that point, you can forget worrying about buying a duck—you've got bigger problems.

Having successfully cut through the clutter means that you've got unifying principles and brand standards in all of your messaging. The links here cannot be tenuous; you can't cross your fingers and hope that customers will stick with an overly obtuse advertisement to get to the bottom of what it is that you're selling. I often point to the famous "smashability" work[1] that was done for Coca-Cola by the Root Bottling Company, which designed a bottle that could be recognized immediately as the iconic brand in the dark (by touch alone!) and also when smashed. If the brand was recognizable even if the product's form was rendered unrecognizable, if you'll pardon the pun, as far as brand standards go, they were crushing it.

If you're helming a brand that's significantly smaller than Coca-Cola—most of us are—it can be easy to look at this information with a healthy dose of skepticism. *Of course it's easy for Coke*, you might think. *I could do it, too, if I had that kind of money behind my campaigns.* But this isn't about money; at least, it doesn't have to be. Instead, it's about isolating a strategy and applying that strategy consistently over time. Consistency is the key here, and that doesn't cost any extra.

The idea of applying standards across a brand's materials—its internal and external corporate identity—is, at its core, just another way of reinforcing identity. Creating a basic style guide or brand standards guide will go a long way toward making this a seamless process across all materials. That way, when new campaigns or sub-brands come up in the future, you can be sure that you (or the agency you're using for your marketing/branding/advertising needs)

---

[1] http://www.coca-colacompany.com/stories/the-story-of-the-coca-cola-bottle/

In the case that any of these questions are answered in the negative, the next step is then to look at how those tools can be realigned or discontinued as necessary. We worked with a health-care company that was getting significant traffic to its website (a tool), but was not successful in converting that traffic to customers. Our audit discovered that, in addition to adjusting the site's message as well as look and feel, the site needed to be restructured for conversion rate optimization (CRO). By adjusting the website to show the sign-up process in three simple steps, we were able to "hold the visitor's hand" and lead them to a conversion. This is often the case—tools can be adjusted to become more effective for converting the customers, ultimately giving you a better return on your investment in the tool itself.

What's The Plan?

Just as you wouldn't start a journey without a map to your destination, you should never go into building a brand without a clearly defined plan or campaign. A clearly defined plan operates on two levels—internal and external—and is informed by the overarching principles that you've outlined in thinking about your identity and the identity of your customers. And in order to truly be effective, a plan needs to be holistic, encompassing numerous platforms—print, web, television, outdoor, direct, and on and on. The way I like to think of marketing is not as one single action, but rather a collaboration of dedicated strategic efforts executed with frequency. It's all-encompassing, a wide and varied approach that makes use of best practices, new technologies, and proven methods that work in harmony with who your brand is and who your customers are.

An integrated plan also cuts down on much of that terrifying guesswork that puts people off marketing in the first place. It's the path that you can clearly navigate rather than getting lost in the "mystery of marketing." When you've got objectives broken down by specific time frames, you have goals to go after, markers by which to judge performance. Instead of flailing around trying to market while blindfolded, you can hit your targets with better accuracy and confidence.

A successful marketing plan will cut out the vagaries and home in on specifics. It lays out a structured plan with step-by-step implementation so that you can clearly see what you're doing on a day-by-day basis. You'll have daily, bi-weekly, weekly, monthly, quarterly, seasonal, and annual goals and objectives, all laid out on a calendar. You'll have an overview of which tools are being deployed when—whether it be your newsletters, social media posts, print collateral, and so on. Your budget for each category will be clearly defined, and you'll have specific strategies for each of your target segments. You'll have strategies that fall into the traditional external marketing realm (radio, TV, Yellow Pages, magazines, billboards, newspapers, direct mail, etc.) and the non-traditional (Facebook, digital ads, SEO, sponsorships). You'll have internal marketing strategies, including signage, blogs, satisfaction surveys, follow-up strategies, and so on.

We'll get into this a little more as the book goes on, but one of the most helpful things about having a plan is having the ability to track your performance and measure your progress. With a plan, you're able to make first downs. You're able to look down the field and see how far you've come—and how much farther you've got still to go before your touchdown. Without a plan, you might as well just be running in circles, expending all your energy but never having a clear view of how far you're getting. And that might be fine for getting your cardio in, but you'll never win the game that way.

Creating your marketing plan is the best thing that you can do for your brand. If you're not sure where to start, visit our site for valuable resources and techniques:

www.dontbuyaduck.com/bonus or text DUCK to 58885.

CHAPTER FOUR

Knowing the Territory— Who's Your Market? Who's the Competition?

I f this chapter title sounds like something out of Sun Tzu's *Art of War* to you, well, it's not an entirely unintended coincidence. In that well-known tome, he warns us: "If you know the enemy and know yourself, you need not fear the result of a hundred battles. If you know yourself but not the enemy, for every victory gained you will also suffer a defeat. If you know neither the enemy nor yourself, you will succumb in every battle."

I'm more of a peaceful guy, but I have to say that the advice is just as applicable on the battlefield of branding as it was when he wrote it in ancient China. From where I'm sitting, the same things

could be said of due diligence and market research, which enable you to understand, first, the environment you're selling in, the product you're selling, who you're selling to, and why they should buy from you. To *very loosely* paraphrase Bill Withers (a musician this time instead of a militarist): "Who are you (and what are you to them)?"

As long as I've been doing this, I'm still surprised by how few companies really proactively researched these areas. I can come up with plenty of examples of how companies have *reactively* done research—scrambled at the last minute (or, to be honest, long after the last minute) to get the low-down on a competitor or to figure out what makes their customers tick. It's common when there's a decrease in business or there's an uptick in direct competition to start looking around for a better strategy; unfortunately, my feeling (and I know Sun Tzu would agree with me) is that if you've neglected to anticipate your competition, you're already getting farther and farther away in their rearview mirror.

Knowing The Environment

If you're in a startup situation, you absolutely need to be paying attention here. But even if you're a small- to mid-size business with a sizable footprint in your area, you can't afford to get blindsided when it comes to the lay of the land.

Getting caught flat-footed and without any read on the competition is an extremely dangerous place to be. You can't anticipate *everything*, of course, but if you're well armed with enough information about your competition and the landscape you're entering into, you're able to take more risks, and more calculated risks at that.

When I start on a project, I usually put together a report on the top ten to twenty competitors in the region. Looking at information

like company history, size, mission, values, and key services, I can start to build a profile of each competitor. What promotions and campaigns have they run in the last 3 to 5 years? What type of media do they utilize? If you're thinking I'm advising you to do this so that you can successfully ape their strategy, you'd be wrong. Rather, I'm advocating knowing the competitor inside and out, understanding as much about what they're doing and why they're doing it. It's not enough to know that they blog; I want to know *why* they're blogging. What kind of audience reach do they have? What kind of response are they getting?

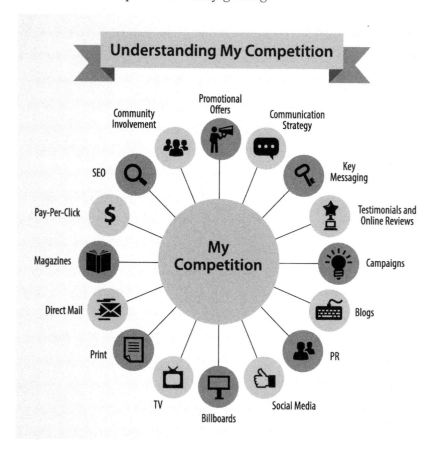

By building this competitive analysis, you can get a clearer overview of where you might fit, what your own unique value proposition is. You can proactively assess whether there's space for you in the marketplace, and whether there is an unfilled niche or an unmet need that you can tailor your mission to. By having this analysis at hand, you can easily anticipate from whence you might see competition coming in, proactively build loyalty with existing customers and get a head start on new customers, creating the narrative of why your brand is different, why they should begin with and continue to choose you. Because I have news for you: if you feel like you don't have competition, you need to buckle up—this means you're the trailblazer (Uber vs. Lyft, McDonalds vs. Burger King) and you need to stay on top of your game.

Bottom line: a competitive analysis is a must for every business. If you haven't done one, you should do one now. If you have yet to launch a product or company, you should move it to the top of your to-do list.

Knowing The Target

While bigger brands certainly have superstar research firms at their beck and call, just because you're running a smaller ship doesn't mean that you can't put in the legwork to become well informed in your own right. There's the obvious adventures in data-mining: background reports, credit reports, lists, directories, censuses—you get the drift. But it's just as easy to do secondary research as a small company, particularly in unexpected places! For example, one of my clients was a player in the hunting apparel industry trying to gain more market share. By digging into publicly

available documents from the U.S. Fish and Wildlife Service,[1] we were able to gain a more comprehensive understanding of another important piece of the puzzle: our target customer. This in-depth census survey would have cost us something in the neighborhood of six figures if we were to put a team on assembling the primary research in-house. That's a considerable savings—and a wonderful treasure trove of data to boot.

By researching your ideal customer's education level, lifestyle, income range, and other data, you'll be in a better position to align yourself with their interests and passions. And you don't have to spend your entire marketing budget on the research, either; there are existing case studies and examples that you can tap into.

Just as you can put together a profile on your competition, you need to put together a profile on your consumer. Their age, gender, career, income level, buying patterns, marital status, ethnicity, political and religious affiliation, and more. Sometimes, you'll find that what seemed like a terrific idea just doesn't have the right location based on that data. A luxury resort located in an area with a sky-high unemployment rate and streets full of abandoned, foreclosed properties is probably not going to do well. It's an understatement to say this would be a good thing to figure out *before* you've broken ground on an 18-hole course with a distinctly resort vibe.

Finally, truly knowing your target market means that you'll be able to tailor messaging and communication properly. If you're a bank with locations in both rural and urban areas, chances are, your target markets are going to have some dissonance—the

---

[1] https://www.census.gov/prod/2012pubs/fhw11-nat.pdf

needs will be different in both, so your messaging shouldn't be one-size-fits-all, either. And never be afraid to uncover too much information. While there's a danger in letting yourself pile up data for data's sake, no harm comes from examining what that data tells us. I remember when my firm once uncovered data showing that retooling an anti-smoking campaign to aim it at the loved ones rather than the smokers would be more effective. It wasn't what we had expected, and the campaign took some reworking, but the end result was worth it, because we were communicating more effectively with a target that was motivated to respond.

Knowing Why They'll Buy

Another part of knowing the target is understanding why that target market would buy from your company. What is it that makes your service, your product, and your business model different from the competition?

Like many elegant and simple solutions, there's one sitting in front of you if you find yourself sitting in the dark when it comes to customer motives. Instead of spinning your wheels and looking to outside sources, why don't you just do something truly revolutionary and ask the customer? While the big box stores have no problem inundating consumers with email after direct mail after social buzz after phone call, small- to medium-size businesses seem to be a little shy about deploying these tactics. Either they're worried about intruding or wearing off their goodwill with their customer, or they're too focused on their product—what has made them great in the past. In today's marketing world, you have to be a little more proactive. You can't abuse the consumer's trust and have them send you straight to the junk folder, but you can't ignore them, either.

So, you have to ask the customer what they want, and why they want it. You can do this through online surveys, in-person surveys, informal surveys, and follow-up offers. You've got more direct points of contact than ever before, thanks to social media and mobile technology. You should be tapping those capabilities for all they are worth.

What's more, there's an unbelievably positive side effect to this direct approach to understanding your customers' motives: you build a relationship based on personal attention and two-way communication. You send a message that your brand cares about its customers, that it listens to them. You grow from that information, and their respect for you will grow as you act on it. Loyalty is no longer a given in today's world; it's easier than ever before to find a replacement service or product, a better price, a faster pathway, or a more responsive customer service department. Keeping an open connection with your customer—being in tip-top customer service mode at all times—is a necessity.

This is particularly useful when you find yourself in a saturated marketplace. Because of our proximity to the headquarters of Walmart, my agency is all too familiar with the urgent need to differentiate. I knew I'd really have to figure out what made my clients tick in order to stand out in a field crowded with big vendors. By building loyalty with our existing clients and finding a clear pathway to future clients, we were able to come into our own niche occupation by offering to be the quarterback of a client's entire media campaign. Some agencies handle digital, some handle social, some handle traditional—we saw that to differentiate ourselves from our competitors, we'd have to find a way to handle it all in a seamless, efficient way. And it helped us stand out in a place where we could have easily gotten lost otherwise.

Partially owing to today's technology, tending to your consumers can mean making adjustments in *real time* to your offerings and your communications. When I lived in Los Angeles, I worked for an agency that served largely high-end automobile clients. We conducted elaborately orchestrated on- and off-road test drives, had access to prototypes years before production, and had the luxury of big budgets and access to test drivers who were outfitted with hand-held devices and could give us detailed responses. We were able to collect and report this real-time data to the engineers, and also use it for our marketing purposes. A small- to mid-size business isn't going to have those perks, but with the customer top of mind, keeping an eye always on what the value of the product is and why they would want to buy it, you're going to be able to be a lot more responsive and unique in your positioning efforts.

Want an amazing shortcut to building a profile of your competition? Join our Business Leadership Series where we discuss this (and other amazing topics that will help you build your business). Request a special invitation by visiting: www.DontBuyADuck.com/bonus or text DUCK to 58885.

CHAPTER FIVE

If Your Marketing Is Not Going According To Plan… Maybe It's Because You Don't Have a Plan!

We've all had that feeling before: we're trying our hardest, but nothing is turning out quite like we wanted it to. Sometimes, we've done all our due diligence, and chance is really all there is to blame. More often than not, though, there's something else at play—something simpler: *we don't have a plan.*

We've all been there, too! Contrary to what you (or your board, or your boss…) might be telling yourself when things aren't going quite right, neglecting to plan doesn't mean that you've got some fatal organizational flaw that is forever going to keep you down. It's totally understandable: as decision makers, we have a *lot* going on, and sometimes we're tasked with changing direction quickly.

Sometimes it feels like, while we've been successful, we are often too busy to find the perfect time to stop and make a plan.

You know me by now, though; I'm a bit of an optimist. I'm here to tell you that it's always possible to plan. That creating a roadmap based on your understanding of your customers, your competition, and your talents and limitations is the surefire way to getting from point A to B. Even if you feel like you're too busy to stop and plan, it's not an impossible task to set that time aside now, saving you time later. In fact, that you've probably got a lot of goodwill and momentum out there ready and waiting for you to harness it. Step one, though: you build the plan.

Building an Integrated Marketing Plan

When I say I want you to have a plan, I'm not just talking about *any* plan, although if you're starting from scratch I don't want you to think that any idea is too small to get things going. But more specifically, the type of plan that's going to help you be able to consistently execute, measuring and making meaning of your results along the way, is an integrated marketing plan.

For so many businesses, even those that have been at the top of their field for a while, it's a real "aha" moment when I show them an example of an integrated plan. Looking at the whole puzzle in full view makes it easy to understand how the pieces fit together, each step supplementing the next. Though this isn't the entire plan— there's more nuts and bolts when you start breaking it down—this top-down visual is a highly relatable high-level picture of every single initiative and touch point with their audience base.

And when I say *every* initiative, I mean it! We're talking an at-a-glance map encompassing their website, their print, their radio, their online strategies, their reputation management, their grassroots campaigns, their PR strategies and partnerships. All of these points are connected to an ultimate purpose, a hub: the objectives at the center of a company's marketing efforts. By seeing this from all sides, all at once, all messages, all channels—be they traditional or social, DIY or designed to the hilt—can be evaluated on whether or not they are aligned to accomplish marketing objectives. At a glance, this visual gives you a cohesive overview of how these components are working together for a singular purpose. Too often, even with skilled companies, we will see when looking at the integrated marketing campaign that there are disjointed campaigns or singular campaigns that don't reach customers at multiple test points. Those campaigns can be effective in their own right if they are there to direct quick traffic, but in terms of building brand awareness and attracting new customers for the long haul, you really need to have a clear and cohesive vision.

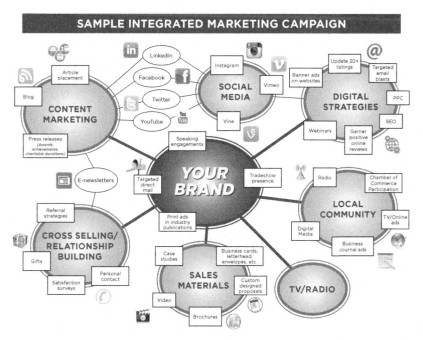

As you can see, having message continuity and an integrated campaign doesn't mean that you can't have multiple channels; it just means that what's appearing on those channels shouldn't feel disjointed or marooned off in the distance from your other messages. It's perfectly fine to have a radio campaign that drives traffic to a call center, or a social campaign that ends up encouraging a phone call. Customers may need multiple points of contact, and it's not always so simple as creating conversions with a single click. But where there's message continuity, there's eventually brand recognition and trust. Where there's confusion across multiple channels, that's when things can start to feel a little off kilter.

Case Study: Tasty Texts

Using consistent messages across appropriately applied tools is a strategic way to find relevancy, even in a crowded market (consistency, which you should be practicing anyway, is always a must when you're trying to stand out in a crowd—it's easier to get lost in the background noise otherwise). When you've got a plan and you follow it consistently, you're almost never going to wind up buying a duck (sorry, Quackers).

In this case, the client was an existing restaurant group trying to break into a new market and stand out from the crowd with brand awareness and new customer acquisition. The singular action that they wanted to pursue was to get phone numbers of new and potential customers. There were follow-up actions, of course—plans to gain business and retain it—but the primary action that everything was pointed toward was getting that contact information. So we had consistently crafted radio, social, and television campaigns that drove home the text campaign, where they'd have to text a number to get a coupon to claim a free appetizer.

That initial engagement gave us a clear starting point to work from: the potential customers were curious. We also had another tool at our disposal now, whether or not the customers followed up with a visit to the restaurant, coupon in hand: we had their phone number. From there, we could then follow up, depending on the level of that engagement. We had a clear picture of what we were trying to accomplish; we had timelines and guidelines to prompt us in the days, weeks, and months to come to continue to push onward with our integrated campaign.

While the concept of this campaign was successful, I'm not going to steer you astray by telling you that you'll always get what you want. That's not going to always happen. But having a marketing plan allows you to keep on track and keep to strategic decision-making even when emotions (such as disappointment) are running high. When you have a plan, you have objectives, and you have purpose and intentionality behind all that you do.

A final word about the benefit of planning: sometimes, planning can actually help spontaneity, too. It puts you in the frame of mind to capitalize on opportunities to connect to your audience, to bring in those customers. Think about how if you have just bought a white Cadillac, you might start to notice white Cadillacs everywhere on the road. You can experience the same thing with recognizing opportunities in marketing: when you've made a plan (the "purchase," in this case), you will start to see opportunities that fit with the objectives of that plan. And this isn't spontaneity without strategy, either; because you're staying on message and on point, these new ideas should fit easily into that framework, too.

Setting Measurable (and Realistic) Goals: Where Do You Want to Go?

Once you've drawn the integrated map, another important step in building a bulletproof marketing plan is to set measurable goals. Depending on the business you're in, these goals can get very specific—and that's good. In fact, the more specific you can get about your goal, the more likely it is that it's a *realistic* one. If you get too pie-in-the-sky about things, which is always fun (and scarily easy to fall into doing), you can easily overreach or get distracted.

Some examples of goals (and again, these aren't one-size-fits-all) might be to aim for an increase in revenue broken down by quarter, demographic, or location (depending on the size and scale of the business). You might want to set a goal to get a certain number of referrals or inquiries (if you don't have inquiries, then you know your external marketing campaign isn't working, and you need to go back to the drawing board). You might want to reach to open a certain number of new locations, to add a specific number of employees. All of these goals can be helpful to a marketer looking to get leads, reach certain sales quotas, and much more.

The more specific the goals are, the easier it is to identify the most appropriate channels and tools to reach those goals. If your goal is to gain a certain amount of followers on your social platforms, you'll know to invest time and energy in making those pages and feeds pop. And the more measurable your goals are, the easier it is to mark your progress and hold your time accountable.

But goals don't need to just be measurable to be useful; that's only half of winning the race. The other half is making sure that your goals are actually *reasonable* (again, brainstorming big plans is all great fun, but you can't take your wishful thinking to the bank). So how do you go about setting a reasonable goal? One way is to look at your resources and your budget—those are pretty finite numbers, and in this economy, even the big players don't have as much wiggle room as they'd like. So that's one way. But as for the rest of your plan, in a move that should come as no surprise to you, I'm going to recommend benchmarks and research wholeheartedly in this particular area. This list is by no means exhaustive, but some proven ways of setting reasonable goals are:

- Looking at the history of your company. What does the data tell you? When you had spikes in your business growth, were there unique events linked to those spikes? What about the lulls—what was happening there?
- Looking at the industry standards. What are other companies around you doing? What about other markets in the same industry—what are those trends telling you?

When you examine this data—yours and your competitors'—try to see it without judging yourself too harshly. The key here is to set a *reasonable* goal; in your current state, that's probably not happening. If you decide your goal really is to be able to run a half marathon, it's entirely possible—you'll just need to take some intermediate training steps, and make sure to leave yourself plenty of time and room for improvement along the way.

When you determine some of these benchmarks, using them to set reasonable goals, you can really start to reach for and understand progress (or lack thereof). If a goal is both reasonable and measurable, you'll be able to feel the jolt of hitting it, or of falling short.

Otherwise, time—and potential revenue—can start slipping away from you.

Making Your Mark: Brand Strategy and Campaign Approach

Aligning your objectives, creating measurable goals, and drawing yourself a map for course-correction when necessary serve to both further and draw from your brand strategy—it's a kind of chicken-and-egg situation I can get behind. Like mapping out the integrated plan, it's important to have an all-encompassing and yet easy-to-understand brand strategy.

It may sound unwieldy, but really, it's as simple as starting a document that houses the core of your brand, what your brand is really about. In this document, you're answering questions such as:

- What is your niche in your industry?
- What is the internal company mission?
- How do you want to be perceived?
- What are some of the attributes that you want associated with your brand?
- What kind of tone do you want to take in your messages?
- What's your brand promise?
- How do you have competitive advantage?
- What are your core competencies?

All of which are meant to help you distill your company down to an essence that can be clearly communicated first of all within your organization and, second, to the customers. It's another layer of assurance that everything you do will be aligned with the clear purpose that you've set out from the very start, and I've found it works no matter what business you're in, be it education, dental, medical, banking, or something else. The main thing is that you've got this guiding document to work from.

Once that brand document is in place, you can check each and every decision that you make against the values it set forth. The brand document should be your guide when you're asking yourself:

- How does this decision align with and reflect upon the brand's core values?
- What is the relevancy of this decision to each of the target market segments? Will that decision impact each of those segments positively or negatively?
- How does this decision, initiative, product, etc. add value to our brand? To our marketing campaigns?

And if the answer to any of these questions is that the decision *doesn't* add value or *doesn't* align with the brand principles, well, just leave that duck at the yard sale and keep on driving.

Similarly, you can use your brand document to refine your approaches to each campaign for each market segment. If your target market is 20-year-olds and you fancy yourself to be a young, hip company with young, hip values, you probably don't want to go with direct mail for a campaign approach—you'll want to look into social or digital. Likewise, if you're looking for customers with a little more money and you're advertising a high-end service, you're going to want to do some thinking about where those customers get their information, and what their habits are. And, like bumpers in a bowling lane that protect the ball from hitting the gutters, the brand document is there to set you up for success, making sure that all of the elements of every campaign—no matter for which market segment—are in alignment with your overall mission. Along the way, you'll get a chance to re-evaluate and remove any Band-Aid or quick fix initiatives that might be costing you some strikes.

SWOTT: Don't Forget the Extra T!

In some communities, SWOTT (or SWOT, as it can be known)—an analysis of strengths, weaknesses, opportunities, threats, and trends (I add the extra T)—is a business principle that can seem like old hat. You can't get a bank loan without one, for instance; your business plan won't seem complete unless you give your investors an idea of these major touchstones.

In marketing, it's not always a given. But when it comes to building your marketing plan, I want you to think of it as *essential*. We've talked before about the role that research and preparation can play in creating a solid foundation for any strategy, and it's certainly no different here. By identifying your strengths, weaknesses, opportunities, threats, and trends—some of which we dug into in our earlier chapters—you'll be several steps ahead of someone who hasn't gone out to honestly survey the terrain yet. The key word there is *honestly*—don't give in to the temptation to stick your head in the sand. If you know you have a high turnover rate, say so. If you know your product has had some complaints in the testing phase, don't try to sweep it under the rug. Remember, we're after bedrock, not Band-Aids.

By ruthlessly pursuing an acute awareness of who you are, how you can be better, who your competitors are, and how you can gain market share, you're ensuring not only that you win big, but that your customer does, too. And that's a brand value I know a consumer can get behind.

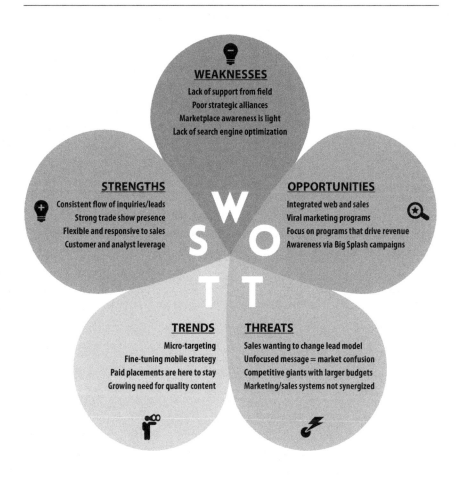

Brand Awareness and New Customer Acquisition

Last, but certainly not least, an integrated marketing plan includes a thorough exploration of external opportunities for building brand awareness. All those PR gurus out there—this piece is for you! We know that segmentation and data and schedules and frequency (which we'll get to in Chapter 8) are all extremely important pieces of the puzzle. But if nobody knows who you are, even the most meticulous marketing planning can be for naught.

When I have clients build their plan for awareness and new customer acquisition, I have them brainstorm every possible target segment and how the client is going to reach them, be that through traditional drivers (direct mail, television) or non-traditional drivers (SEO, pay-per-click). The traditional drivers are often more like a megaphone to a wider audience, whereas the non-traditional drivers can be targeted with a more specific message to a specific niche. This combines with other standard PR measures: a social media presence and strategy, pathways to contribute content and thought leadership throughout the community (guest blogging, expert commentary on a current trend piece in the media, etc.), cross-promotional partnerships with complimentary products and services, and finally goodwill-generating efforts of genuine social responsibility. All of these contribute to what we call your company's "blue sky value," which takes into account your reputation and brand recognition in addition to your physical assets. And PR can net you some considerable goodwill and traction with your audience and community, particularly when it comes to reinforcing your values. If you're a brand that claims to be honest and caring, a good community citizen, for instance, then partnerships and charity events that promote those values are going to be treated as more authentic.

It's a long ingredient list, but it's a proven one. Sit down, mix well, and see where things go from here.

To the outsider, an integrated marketing plan can look like an overwhelming juggernaut. Become an immediate insider by downloading our planning tool, it'll make integrated marketing plans seem like child's play and make you look like a marketing genius. Visit: www.DontBuyADuck.com/bonus or text DUCK to 58885.

CHAPTER SIX

Internal Marketing:
It's What's on the Inside That Counts

I keep talking about debunking the mystery of marketing and empowering you to be less fearful (or reactive) and more forceful (and intentional) when it comes to devising and executing a marketing strategy. And part of that is really distilling the concept down to a simple definition. In the case of marketing, this simple definition enables us to talk about a lot of complicated things wrapped up in a friendly, easy-to-digest format.

As I see it, marketing is any and every interaction that anyone has with your brand. From the tiniest tweet to the largest launch, every connection with a customer represents an opportunity to be seized. And studies have shown us that not all connections are equal, nor are all customers. We'll go over some data later that points to the importance of satisfying current customers over acquiring new ones, for instance. It's simply easier to sell to someone who has already had a positive brand interaction—or, at base level, a brand awareness—than it is to connect with someone who hasn't. And it doesn't take a seasoned marketing guru to extrapolate that it's important to make sure that the interactions that your brand is having with these consumers are positive ones!

Like the first impressions you give and gather as individuals within society, the impressions that these customers have of your brand are equally important, not to mention equally quick to form. So just as you might often spend time in the barber's chair getting a close shave and a haircut in preparation for a first job interview, where first impressions can make or break a relationship (a potential employer has no reason to call you back in if you've failed to capture their interest), it follows that marketers should spend a little time looking not just in the mirror at how your brand presents itself, but *inside* the organization as well. Because if you're all style and no substance, there's no amount of slick sales trickery you can pull to make someone think otherwise.

Look Within to Build a
Better Customer Experience

Before you spend a cent on anything external—campaigns, consultants, etc.—you need to take a long hard look within your organization to ensure that you've got your internal marketing (that is, marketing for customers already in your pipeline) optimized. When I'm talking to a client, if they tell me they've got some terrific retention rate—say, 80% or so—I'd probably tell them that it looked as if their internal house was in order. A retention rate that is high means that when they've hooked customers, those customers are sticking around. That means that client could be confident in moving forward with new customer acquisition.

However, for many clients, it takes a little longer to get it right. If the retention rate is lower, down around 20 to 30%, I'd be more inclined to slow things down and take a good, long look at what's going on inside the brand. If 70 to 80% of your customers are leaving after their initial contact, it's probably a good sign that something on the inside isn't quite functioning at maximum efficiency.

When I'm talking about looking inside, I'm talking about a top-to-bottom exam. The reason for your retention problems could be stemming from an overarching issue (lack of clarity in your messages or your mission), or it could be the smallest thing (a customer service representative who isn't putting your organization's best face forward on routine phone calls). I've been surprised—and then not so surprised—at some of the audits I've run where I've found that the tiniest point of connection is, in fact, the sticky wicket when it comes to excellent customer service and customer retention.

My point is that no boulder is too large and no pebble too small to go unturned; this is particularly true when it comes to making sure that your staff, and I mean everyone from the cubicles to the C-level, is adequately equipped to represent your brand in its very best light. Advertising is one thing, messaging is one thing, but the authenticity and importance of brand ambassadorship that should radiate from your staff is what will enable you to stand out from the rest of the competition. Without it, you can bet you'll be stumbling behind, throwing good money after bad. Even the best strategy can start to look a little like Quackers if your house isn't in order.

The good news is, there isn't a barrier to promoting buy-in internally. You can start by simply reinforcing your mission and vision within your company culture. Make sure that the people who answer the phones understand the values you laid out in your marketing plan. Make sure your vendors and outside partners are treated just as well as you'd want to treat your customers. Ensure that adequate staff training is in place to bring everyone into alignment with the values, the tone, the approach, everything that makes up your brand. Brand ambassadors are some of the best advertising you'll ever get—living, breathing embodiments of all of the great qualities that set your company apart.

Cultivating (and Engaging) Ambassadors Online: Now More Than Ever

There's no doubt that promoting positive brand ambassadorship within and outside of any organization has been and will always be a critical component to success. But this has never been true so much as it is in this moment. Facebook, Twitter, Yelp, even boilerplate listings with ratings picked up by web crawlers—there's never been a time when there's been more user- and third-party-generated content available to consumers, often instantaneously and in real time. Whereas before, a bad customer review might take a while to trickle down into the outside world—and even then, only if it was borne of a particularly egregious infraction—customer complaints can easily go viral nowadays. It's not all doom and gloom; compliments and kudos can just as easily get liked, linked, and shared, too.

It's amazing how the conversation around social media has changed in the past few years. We've gone way past the decision point of whether or not to participate in creating or curating an online presence. The auto-population of information on websites, coupled with the fact that consumers have more avenues to express their thoughts and experiences directly and without mediation, it's happening whether we like it or not. And when it comes to maintaining an online presence (yes, even if you *think* you don't have one—you do!), it's preferable to play an active role in that presence. People are talking; you should be a part of the conversation.

This doesn't mean that you can stop people from sharing their less-than-shiny anecdotes, or from Tweeting out complaints to hundreds of followers in the wake of a disappointing interaction. I'm not advocating the kind of totalitarian approach that would have you deleting all unfavorable comments from Facebook or blocking any critical commenters from your blog. What I am advocating is harnessing the power of these populist avenues to reinforce the values of your brand.

Customer complaint happening? Help solve it in public, and in real time. Talk to your audiences, engage with your customers. Be helpful. Be genuine. And when you can't solve a problem, make your most earnest effort to *hear* them and be empathetic. Empathy goes a long way—in life and in business. Sometimes, knowing that someone is listening is all it takes to diffuse a naysayer. Sometimes it's a lot more complicated than that. But no matter the context, positive or negative, these interactions are always moments in which you can proactively shape perception, creating and engaging brand ambassadors in the process.

That's a lot more productive than throwing up your hands and turning off your monitor, I promise.

Make New Friends, But Keep the Old: Retaining Existing Customers

I'm going to take off my marketer hat for a minute, and I want you to take off yours, too. Let's talk consumer to consumer. Person to person.

Have you ever given your hard-earned dollars to a company, even going so far as to sign a contract for service that binds you together for better or worse for a couple years? Only to feel forgotten when someone better—mostly, *newer*—comes along?

A cell phone contract (and many other service-related contracts, for that matter) isn't marriage, of course. But it *is* something that can cost the consumer a pretty penny, and it's not fun to watch as you turn on the television or open up a web page and see ad after ad racing to give *newer* customers better deals than you got.

Loyalty is something to be rewarded, and while many companies pay lip service to this concept in their communications, their follow-through is often a little lacking. I know I don't enjoy feeling like I'm a replaceable commodity as a consumer; I bet you feel the same. When companies favor new customers over building on their loyal base, they're making a big mistake, and leaving a considerable amount of money (not to mention goodwill) on the table. A 2013 study[1] called "Global Insights on Succeeding in the Customer Experience Era" done by Oracle noted that "Ninety-seven percent of executives agree that delivering a great customer experience is

---

[1] http://www.oracle.com/us/corporate/press/1903222.

critical to business advantage and results, and respondents estimate that the average potential revenue loss for not offering a positive, consistent and brand-relevant customer experience is 20% of annual revenue."

What I see too often is that these existing customers are taken for granted, rather than taken care of. While it may seem that pushing to acquire new customers is the only way to grow business, a huge part of making sure your internal housekeeping is in order and optimized is ensuring that the customers in your system are prioritized appropriately. Not only do they provide valuable resources in the form of referrals, brand ambassadorship, and goodwill, they are a *considerably* more cost-effective resource on which to concentrate your time and energy. This can be hard to put a dollar amount on, but the value is undeniable; Bain and Company famously reported that it costs six to seven times more to acquire a new customer than to retain an existing one.

Staying on top of your internal marketing means putting a high priority on these existing customers. You'll want to make sure you're doing a thorough and consistent job with collecting their information at all points: email, mailing address, phone number. Drive them to your website, and to your social sites. Think about what creative promotions (again, back to the marketing plan!) you can implement to entice existing customers to provide more information and to promote points of contact. And once they're solidly in your system, take care of them while they're there. Don't forget to ask your customers how they're doing; follow through with following up. People are usually willing to give you their opinion, and by asking them proactively, you're showing that you do care. See what you can do in the way of implementing clear pathways to customer service, or member benefits that really shine. You can't fake true loyalty—and after all, your loyal customers won't bother to!

The Extra Mile: Making the Most of Upselling, Cross-Promotion, and Referrals

Some marketing initiatives are budget busters. That's fine for the big guys who can pull out the big guns, but not so much for the small- to medium-size companies that I represent on a daily basis. In fact, I think this is part of what makes marketing in general so fear-inducing, particularly when it comes to startups. If you've only got a small pool of money to work with and no room for error, the thought of buying a duck is understandably terrifying!

But one of the wonderful things about an organized and optimized internal marketing strategy is that so many of the initiatives you can take are far from cost-prohibitive. With a commitment to clear communication and a synergistic point of view, you can often maximize your efforts with minimal cost. Maintaining an effective relationship with your existing customer base is one of the ways this can happen; you've already gotten them in the door, you don't have to worry about the cost of that again. Another way is by making the most of your referrals, upselling your services, and cross-selling with promotional partners where appropriate.

I once had a financial services firm that I was working with whose breadth and depth of services were truly remarkable. Not only did they offer financial advising and accounting services, but they worked with attorneys of all stripes along with management consultants, tax specialists, and more.

At first glance, these guys were doing everything right. But when we dug in to see how things were looking under the hood, I could see a few places where it would behoove them to take advantage of their full stable of services and connections. Upon surveying customer feedback, it became clear that the customers of one branch of the firm's service were often unaware of the other branches; a client who used the firm's tax specialty services had contracted a management consultant from a management consulting firm. According to a study from Marketing Metrics, "the probability of selling to an existing customer is 60 to 70%," whereas "the probability of selling to a new prospect is 5 to 20%." Knowing this, I advised the firm to put some heft behind its communication with current clients across all services, making sure that they could hear, loud and clear, that there was more to the firm than they knew about. After implementing effective cross-pollination strategies, the firm was also able to align all of its different specialists and service providers on the same page, too; upselling and cross-selling were added to everyone's mental checklist at no extra cost to the firm.

This is to say nothing of the considerable connections that the firm had within other sectors of the business community. Although they didn't employ architects, for example, they had connections to some of the best in their market. By approaching their specialists' external networks, the firm was able to strengthen cross-promotional opportunities in the community as well. Now, they were getting referrals from trusted partners in their community, and vice versa. It was a beautiful *quid pro quo*, one that netted results for little to no cost.

And finally, just like likes and faves and retweets can make more impact than even the most finely crafted glossy magazine ad, referrals from happy customers should be featured front and center in your internal marketing and customer relations strategies. Make sure you have a policy in place for following up on these referrals.

To Keep Customer Relations Strong, Strengthen Internal Communications

Keeping in mind that marketing is, as I said at the start, every single interaction you have with an existing or potential customer, it follows that strengthening internal communications is one surefire way to keep customer relations strong. In your brick-and-mortar operations, this means looking at your in-store signage, your layout, your uniforms, name tags, even your stationery and business cards. You want to make sure you present a unified and friendly front to customers who come in based on advertising that they've seen—whether it was a billboard or a sign in the parking lot, you want their conversion from curious to customer to be seamless, to make sense.

Outside the store, or particularly if you're an online brand, the same kind of consistency should be applied to your e-newsletters, website, email signature, and social media presence. Though it's easy in this day and age to forget about the importance of the telephone, even your on-hold messaging is worth a look. Are you capitalizing on the time you've got a customer on the line, or are you just filling it with endless muzak and repetitive messages? What if you took that same time to educate them about your services, your messages, your values?

If you look at each of these opportunities as a chance to strengthen your customer relationships, you'll no doubt start to find new points of connection. Maybe there's an opportunity for a short customer service survey on the customers' printed receipt.

Maybe there's a follow-up call that could be placed where you could collect feedback. The possibilities are only limited by what you've got the wherewithal and staffing to tackle.

Reputation Management

The final point I want you to consider is something we've already spent some time talking about: reputation management. Just as I didn't mean to scare you by saying that you don't have a choice when it comes to having an online presence, I don't want to put you too on edge here, but the real, honest truth is that you simply *must* have a strategy in place for reputation management. Much of this is done over social networks these days, particularly when it comes to customer feedback. But there's also offline reputation management, in the press and in the day-to-day life of your consumer population. Keep an eye out for those golden testimonials, the rich stories and special experiences that you can share and bring to the forefront. Likewise, because it can't all be sunshine and rainbows, take an honest look at negative stories, too. Your customers will thank you for it.

You also need to remember that in your daily life, you create a digital trail, too. You need to make sure as business owners that these breadcrumbs don't lead negative publicity your way. While it may be hard to resist posting on a public forum such as Facebook or Yelp in an effort to get some attention in a customer service issue, you have to acknowledge that these comments can easily be traced back to you without the distinction having been made between your private life and your public one. Simply put: you are one of the faces of your brand, and you need to act accordingly, even in cyberspace.

Meet and share techniques and solutions with your marketing peers in our Business Leadership Series. Learn (and copy!) from the best practitioners on the ground today. Request an invite by visiting: www.DontBuyADuck.com/bonus or text DUCK to 58885.

CHAPTER SEVEN:

Execution Is Everything—
How You Get From Your Own
5-Yard Line to the End Zone

Even the most cool-headed among us can get overwhelmed when there's a monumental task staring us down. It doesn't matter what it is: an end-of-year financial goal, a marathon, a cavernous closet full of junk that our wives have finally stood up and declared needs to go *immediately*. I'm breaking a sweat just thinking about it.

So. How do you eat an elephant? One bite at a time.

Er, okay. I've always found that adage a little creepy (if not nauseating), so I'll put it another way. I'm a casual football fan, and I love a good football analogy (it's almost like Zen *koans*; there's a football-related saying for every situation). In this case, one of the most overwhelming moments would come when a team has been backed up into its own 5-yard line at fourth down and 10 to go. They've got the entire field in front of them, 100 impossible yards long, not to mention several tons of gnashing teeth and flexing muscle. The QB can see the end zone, but only if he squints.

So. How's he going to get over there?

The answer isn't sexy, but it's simple—one down at a time. No matter how far away those goalposts are, as long as the QB and his team can make the measurable gains they need to within the rules and timeframe of the game, they can keep going until they get there. And just as there have been some great comebacks in the history of football, the intertwined histories of marketing and business are no different. You'll have your own marketing highlight reels—breakaway runs, long passes with spectacular catches—but ultimately, you should be measuring in smaller increments, and working toward first downs all the way to the end zone.

That's where *you* come in, Dear Reader. Those objectives you set up in your marketing plan a few chapters ago? Those are the end zone. All the related elements of your plan—your campaigns, your messages, your internal and external marketing strategy, your social strategy, etc.—those are what's going to drive you forward, yard by yard, as you execute each step until you have the pleasure of spiking that ball into the painted grass at the other end of the field.

Get Started (and Don't Stop!)

As with executing any initiative, getting started is the most important step. You'll never make it to the end zone without that successful first down, and you'll never make the most of your marketing plan if you don't have that get up and go (emphasis on the *go*). And once you've gotten started, you need to *keep going*. It seems like such a simple thing to miss, but you might be surprised how many talented teams with tremendous products that we've worked with who just stopped in their tracks and failed to consistently execute. If you've taken the time to build a clear marketing plan, and you've got objectives to work toward and a path to get there, it's absolutely essential that you keep going. There's a reason why I've been called an execution specialist, and it's because for me, execution (rather than simply talking about things) is everything.

It's especially worth noting the importance of consistency in a day and age where changing strategies is such a common and tempting reaction to difficult times. Companies are constantly changing goals and derailing progress mid-play, be it on a branding effort, a product, or an ad campaign. It's easy to get panicked with real-time feedback and analytics, too; I can completely understand feeling nervous if a campaign didn't do as well as initially predicted, but it's very important to continue applying your initiatives *consistently*, making small adjustments rather than derailing a carefully crafted plan. After all, if you're driving and it starts raining, you don't make a U-turn in the middle of the highway—you just turn on your wipers.

Follow Your Marketing Calendar (Without Fail)

One of the most crucial components of the plan you built is your calendar. Your calendar is your timeline, your guiding star.

You've built it from a list of executable items—your first downs—and those items are doable if you stick to the plan. And once you start making first downs, you keep going forward, tracking and measuring your results appropriately as time goes by. You look at your goals for the week, the month, the quarter, however you've laid it out, and you keep moving down the field.

Sample Marketing Calendar

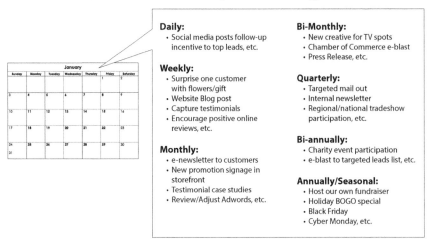

Daily:
- Social media posts follow-up incentive to top leads, etc.

Weekly:
- Surprise one customer with flowers/gift
- Website Blog post
- Capture testimonials
- Encourage positive online reviews, etc.

Monthly:
- e-newsletter to customers
- New promotion signage in storefront
- Testimonial case studies
- Review/Adjust Adwords, etc.

Bi-Monthly:
- New creative for TV spots
- Chamber of Commerce e-blast
- Press Release, etc.

Quarterly:
- Targeted mail out
- Internal newsletter
- Regional/national tradeshow participation, etc.

Bi-annually:
- Charity event participation
- e-blast to targeted leads list, etc.

Annually/Seasonal:
- Host our own fundraiser
- Holiday BOGO special
- Black Friday
- Cyber Monday, etc.

Just as the quarterback is tasked with calling the plays and then executing on each play, the other members of the team shoulder significant responsibility here, too. It's the rare exception, rather than the rule, that the quarterback is able to run the ball from end zone to end zone. When it comes to executing with respect to deadlines and deliverables, nothing ensures success so much as designating a team or team member to be accountable in pushing each task forward.

I've had the pleasure, over the years, of working with a highly respected author and business consultant who has worked with Fortune 500 CEOs and other great executives from coast to coast. He always asks the question: "Who's number one on this?" Make sure that for every objective, every project, every deadline, you've got a quick answer to that question, even if you're working with a small team. I know that it's harder for companies with fewer resources (namely, fewer people) to feel like it's possible to do this, but it can really be as simple as tasking one employee to take point on a project. You don't need a dedicated project manager in your office, but each project has to be managed in a dedicated way. By protecting a team member's bandwidth on each project, you're ensuring that you've got time and energy carved out to keep making those first downs, yard by yard.

The Rewards of Consistency

Tracking your deliverables to your plan has another component, too: making sure that you're consistent in your execution of content. No matter what kind of content you're working with—social media, web design, internal signage and materials—you should be constantly checking for alignment along the way. Using an old logo in an ad campaign? Swap it out! The tone of your social media posts not matching your current language? Rework the language of your posts. Consistency in execution—not just in keeping to your timelines, but keeping aligned to your purpose and values—will give you tangible rewards, and quickly so. If your content marketing is not consistent, that all-important SEO ranking will flounder. Your customers will have to work to remember who you are and what you stand for. But if the opposite is true, if you are a shining example of consistent application of technique, tone, and so on, you're going to stay top of mind. And this need not be done by an unattainable artisanal hand; you can automate to the extent that you can still do so effectively (using technology and schedulers like Hootsuite for after-hours social updates, for example).

Another important consideration is that inconsistency actually looks bad for a brand. If you post only once a month on social media, for example, you can quickly look outdated or out of touch. If you start an e-newsletter or blog and then let it go completely idle for months at a time, it looks bad. Just as you as a consumer might notice when a technology looks dated or sloppily constructed, your consumers are going to notice if you don't follow through on your initiatives. This is especially true of social media, where authentic reactions take place in real time (or close to real time)—while it's fine to go dark overnight, you don't want to let questions or comments linger unanswered for weeks or months on a Facebook wall. When you continue to make gains and track them consistently, you'll enjoy being able to see the progress that you've made quarter by quarter, year by year, and more.

Bottom line: whatever you do, however you do it, do it consistently. Execute each component of your campaign—make each play that your QB calls—with the kind of dogged tenacity and surety that results from having a plan. Go the extra mile with your marketing, don't flag on your standards of excellence, and keep your value statement and overall purpose (and your customer!) in the forefront of everything you do. Make sure to celebrate your successes, because you deserve to. But never take your eye off the end zone. You're going to get there eventually, I know you will.

You need to download the ultimate planning tool—our Marketing Calendar Spreadsheet. This will help you create cohesive marketing plans that will help get your team to the Superbowl (… of Marketing). Visit: www.DontBuyADuck.com/bonus or text DUCK to 58885.

CHAPTER EIGHT

"The Yellow Pages Are Dead!" and Other Lies Businesses Tell Themselves

There's some debating still to be done about the fate of the Yellow Pages. We know that the number of advertisers filling those pages is dramatically slashed each and every day. During the first quarter of 2015, for instance, print revenues had shown a 22% decrease over 2014.[1] We know that it's the rare person who turns to the Yellow Pages before they pull out their smartphone or tablet and fire up a quick Google search.

But the Yellow Pages still do have enduring uses other than advertising. As a poor couple of undergrads, my wife and I used the

---

[1] http://www.marketwatch.com/story/yellow-pages-limited-reports-first-quarter-2015-financial-results-2015-05-08-7173313

hefty volume to level out a sorely sagging used couch that made up the majority of our living room furniture. I'm not the only one who takes advantage of this comic fodder about one of our oldest advertising avenues, either; there's a great sketch by one of my favorite comedians, Pete Holmes, about how the phone book essentially comes to your door like an unwelcome guest, only to stare up at you and say: "Here I am! It's a printed version of the Internet for you to have to throw away!"

But as far as the businesses I work with are concerned, I'm not worried about all that. I'm worried about making sure that every client I talk to gives each and every advertising avenue its proper due, even if it's something as widely dismissed as the phone book. The lie, in this case, isn't so much about the effectiveness of the medium—it's about the willingness to dismiss a potential tool without so much as a second thought.

The Major Players: Lies We Tell Ourselves About Advertising Options

I can absolutely sympathize with what it feels like to have spent money on something that just didn't work. There wasn't anything wrong with Quackers, for example; he was a perfect duck. He just wasn't the thing I needed. The same can be said of many legitimate marketing choices—advertising a service in the Yellow Pages might be a perfectly reasonable thing to do at the outset, but if you're open to examining and adjusting your strategy as you go along, you might find that the time has passed for that method. In this case, the next step should be to examine *why* the method isn't working, rather than just dismissing it out of hand.

For example: if you're advertising a product geared at the 20-something set in the **Yellow Pages**, I'd say, yes, you're probably barking up the wrong tree. But I do have a few clients who still actually bring in business with the printed phone book. If you're trying to reach retirement communities to offer specials on dentures, for instance, this might still be an appropriate tool to do so. The same thing can be said of the **newspaper**, where lawyers might effectively advertise for older clients to join mass tort suits. So much of the adjustments in these and other cases can be made by looking at your target segmentation—revisiting who uses what medium, and what products fit in best where. By committing to researching your options rather than relying on gut reactions or so-called accepted wisdom, you leave yourself the room to discover that it's women over 55 years of age, rather than teenage males, who are primarily driving Facebook usage these days. In fact, digital media accounts for about 29% of all advertising revenues, meaning the audience is far wider than just bored teenagers and college students.[2]

Direct mail is another popular target of derision these days, but like the Yellow Pages and other print media, it has a place in certain marketing plans. I've seen a resurgence in the usefulness of direct mail these days, and a lot of that usefulness hinges upon a client's willingness to make adjustments to their plans that reflect current best practices. The Direct Marketing Association, which produces an annual Statistical Fact Book, posts in its 2015 fact book: "While the total number of direct mail pieces sent out each year has steadily declined over the past decade, there is still great

---

[2] www.alger.com/media/pdf/BReynolds_Transcript_091514.pdf

marketing opportunity with direct mail. Especially as organizations continually learn to better create and target mailings to speak to the individual."

I did a direct mail campaign for a salon in the South that was successful because it was an immediately redeemable offer for a free product with the purchase of service. I've seen direct mail work well when there's a clear target expiration and little fine print. I've also seen it work well for some high-end services, particularly when addressed directly to the consumer by name, rather than "Current Resident." I've seen great response for certain services targeted to newcomers in a neighborhood. So it's not about dismissing direct mail as a concept, it's about ensuring the best approach and promoting the best drivers.

This is true for *any* advertising avenue; I'm not a proponent for one over the other. I truly believe it's not a one-size-fits-all proposition. And although we have wisdom based on experience in developing and managing many campaigns, we begin as a neutral party when confronting any campaign. So while one offer or client might be well served by direct mail, another could be bolstered by a presence on the radio. Radio won't work for all offers, of course, but I have seen proof that it works more than well for some: I have a client who spends $500 a month on a boutique oldies radio station and sees a majority of its queries resulting from that advertising. This client's competitors don't advertise on that radio station, and I can't speak for whether or not what they are doing is working for them, but I *can* tell you that they're spending exponentially more to achieve those results while my client is happily bringing in customers from a relatively small investment on an often-overlooked format.

Just as technology has changed the way we listen to music and the radio (streaming services and satellite subscriptions have supplanted more traditional formats—2014 statistics from BIA Kelsey Sponsored Research estimate that digital radio has grown "to 20 percent of the overall radio advertising market in just a few years"[3]), the same can be said for **network television**. While consumers have more choices than ever before when it comes to curating their viewing experiences (in many cases, cutting commercials or cable packages out of the equation altogether), there's still a case to be made for advertising on network television shows that haven't been affected by streaming and the DVR—live results shows and morning or evening news, for example.

Cable television, though you've got to be selective about your timing and audience, can also still be a winner. Understanding how to correctly implement burst and pulse in your media buys is crucial on cable TV (though cable is not the *only* avenue where this applies; all traditional, and even some non-traditional, advertising avenues can benefit from correctly applying burst and pulse scheduling)—when you first come on to the scene, you'll want to burst in, going for the maximum frequency and distribution that you can, laying the groundwork for your company to be part of a permanent recall in the minds of the viewers. After that point, you can refine your approach, relying on smaller but steady pulses to keep the brand fresh. You can play with your budget in here, too; I know not everyone has millions to work with, and so sometimes by working with your ad reps at the stations you can purchase more

---

[3] http://www.biakelsey.com/BIAKelsey-Sponsored-Research-Internet-Radio-Revolution.pdf

of a shorter-period spot to get the frequency up. Similarly, and in a less traditional medium, you can get more bang for your buck with **Google AdWords** by strategizing on how best to stretch your dollar: buying spots for the search terms that are still popular, but not necessarily #1. Market share is always there for the thorough and the prepared, so long as you don't dismiss an entire category of tools without a second look.

E-blasts and social media are widely popular right now, but that doesn't mean that they aren't without their own detractors, either. Critics point to the ROI and lukewarm reception from audiences on both of those lists; it's easy to opt in, and it's even easier to opt-out—you can hide something from your Facebook feed, and you can instantly filter out emails from which you haven't bothered to click "unsubscribe" (and your company is still paying for those deliveries, by the way). The truth is a little more complicated than that—not all e-blasts and social media marketing campaigns are created equal. If you're having a hard time with either of yours, take a look at what your lists are like, and what offers you're sending out. How do your promotions look and feel? Do they reflect the values of your company? Do they respond to the needs of your customers in specific market segments? Are your lists adequately segmented, curated, and maintained? Are you providing content and offers that are of value to the reader, or are your messages coming across as spam? Are you truly communicating with your customer or simply broadcasting *at* them? These are all questions that can reveal some deficiencies to address—deficiencies that are to blame for less-than-stellar campaigns rather than the mediums themselves.

In the same spirit of collaborative engines and networks like social media are **partnerships** with area businesses or organizations (Can you partner with your local Chamber of Commerce, for example, in an e-blast exchange? What exposure might that net you?), or **grassroots initiatives such as street teams.** While not appropriate for every brand or product, there are times when you just can't beat the power of pounding the pavement and generating buzz with boots on the ground. If poor old Quackers was one of the most influential moments in making me a marketer, the other would have to be my experience marketing my own products from an early age. My parents were part-time touring musicians when I was younger, and I remember being 3 years old, going onstage and "performing" for the first time alongside my brother. Always a student of the game, I started playing in bands by the age 10 (with our parents driving us to showcases and gigs, that old station wagon came in handy again). I was creating my own branding media kits and websites at an early age, and I even applied for a bulk mailing permit at age 18 so that I could mail out several hundred press kits each month. It was slow going at first, but my reputation as a musician and marketer kept me in the game and I continued to explore every tool that could effectively connect my music with the listener.

Several years later, then a young adult, I was recording and performing with a successful band in Hollywood, California, where we were a fixture on the Sunset Strip playing at infamous clubs such as the Whisky a Go-Go, House of Blues, and as a house band at the world-famous Viper Room (back when it was owned by actor Johnny Depp). Eventually, our group went on to have music published on several network TV show soundtracks (such as *Keeping Up With the Kardashians* and several MTV reality shows). During that era, I had an extremely rewarding experience, not just as a musician but as a marketer.

During my band's performance period in Hollywood, we got the opportunity to practice street team guerilla strategies for bringing in an audience in a highly competitive music scene. On any given night, we had to share the stage with many bands, often having to pay to play. We looked for a solution to stand out from the crowd, and we were rewarded by long lines running around the block on Sunset—on a weeknight, no less!

We did this by putting boots on the ground and pounding the pavement. We realized that many international visitors in this tourist destination were not sure *where* to go for entertainment (with so many options in the area), much less *how* to get there (L.A. is notorious for its traffic nightmares, and if you're a tourist with no transportation, good luck to you!). We found something that would help us and our potential listeners: reaching out to the top 10 hostels in the city, landing a deal with six of them to advertise us as American rock music at world-famous clubs—paired with a free ride. We created a sign-up sheet and drove to the hostels on the way to our shows, picking up our own fans. Our band members, our girlfriends, and our groupies pitched in to drive as our demand grew. Eventually, we began renting 15-passenger vans and hiring drivers to handle the demand.

We had a good product. We believed in our product. We wanted our customers to experience the product, so we found out what was important to them and met them there. The solution was actually quite simple, and the reward was creating fans from all over the world who bought merchandise and had a memorable story to share with others about their experience.

This was also a point in my life when I learned that sometimes, particularly when you're just starting out and money is terribly tight, your greatest currency is your time. When you have less money to spend, one of the things you need to look at is your time: how best to use it, how much elbow grease you can put into a product. Get out there in the street. If you're a restaurant, go have some servers walk around samples within a five-mile radius. If you're a musician, get out there and play. If you're a new company on the block, go door-to-door and forge partnerships with neighborhood standards. In my experience, some of the most rewarding—and most fun—marketing efforts have cost the least. But they've always taken time—time, and a lot of love.

Other Lies We Tell Ourselves to Sleep at Night

Although for marketers, a lot of the lies we tell ourselves as businesspeople pertain mostly to advertising avenues, that doesn't mean that we're off the hook even if we *have* done a decent amount of research and haven't broken bad on any one method without just cause. While many of these lies apply to levels you might not work on—engineering, design, etc.—I still wanted to compile a list of lies to watch out for.

In my experience, the biggest offenders have been…

- **"There's nothing out there like my product (or service)!"** Everyone needs to think they are unique. And for the most part, we are! All the products that have ever been made are unique in *some* way, unless they're a direct copy. But here's the thing: while you need to believe in your uniqueness, you also need to understand that there are tons of other smart people out there thinking of these same problems. Don't blindly march forward with a product or service just because *you* think it's going to sell like hotcakes.

- **"My product (or service) is so good, it doesn't need marketing!"** If this one were true, I'd happily be out of business. But it's not. The iPhone is an amazing product, a certified game-changer. You don't see Apple ripping down their billboards, though, do you?

- **"I know my customers and I know what they want."** Unless you're actively surveying your customers' needs and gathering feedback, you can't assume that this is true. Make it a practice to keep in touch with the people who pay your bills.

- **"My customers know all the services I have to offer."** Make sure you shout all your products and services—not just your marquee stuff—from the rooftops. If you're an attorney who partners with a licensed CPA and can get all of your clients' tax needs met in one shot, tell them!

- **"I am tracking my leads well."** Much like knowing your customer, this is something you're going to have to constantly be calibrating.

- **"I just need to ride the technology wave."** No matter how good your tools are, they won't be worth much if you aren't using them correctly. You can't rely on technology as a crutch, nor can you ignore it.

- **"Technology doesn't work for me."** At this point, you don't have a choice. You don't have to use a piece of technology or a certain tool that doesn't work for you, but do yourself a favor and have an open mind enough to find the one that might!

Sometimes you get more than halfway through a book and you still haven't checked the online bonuses. I know this isn't you—you're not a procrastinator. But, for the other guys... check out the site, check out the bonus materials and see how we can help you become even better at growing your business.

Visit: www.DontBuyADuck.com/bonus or text DUCK to 58885.

CHAPTER NINE

Getting Married Is an Emotional Decision, but Marketing Decisions Shouldn't Be

W e each make hundreds of little decisions a day with our head or our hearts or a combination of both. Marriage is a not-so-little decision, of course; choosing a life partner is probably one of the more anxiety-inducing (and amazingly rewarding!) things a person can do. Despite what the more pragmatic among us might say, I'm willing to bet that, for many, it's also a decision that's largely made with the heart, ruled by emotions rather than a clear and logical head. And that's completely understandable. You've met someone; you've felt the butterflies. You've imagined your lives entwined together, what your children might be like—your daughter with her smile and your son with your taste for hijinks. Maybe you've even taken the first step and you're hiding a ring somewhere in a sock drawer. All of this is imbued with undeniable *emotion*. Even when you've got cold feet, weighing the pros and cons of leaving your single life behind, your decisions are driven by emotion: you will be *happier* with her, so you make it to the altar. You *love* her, so you stand by her.

So: not such a small decision, not by any stretch of the imagination.

In our lives as marketers and businesspeople, we must make decisions both big and small every day. And a lot of these, like marriage, end up being made with emotion. Marketing and marriage may seem like an odd comparison, and if you're thinking so—good, you're halfway there! I would argue that emotion definitely has its place in marketing, insofar as you should be passionate about the decisions you make, you should hold your customers in your heart when shaping every product or service you offer, and you should absolutely have that heat within when you're making a connection with your customer, communicating with them, and ultimately helping people in whatever way you've chosen to provide value. But—and you knew there was a but coming, didn't you?—you have to leave your emotions behind when you're making strategic decisions about your marketing.

All too often in business, particularly if the buffer between us and the company is a thin one, such as in startups and small businesses, we let our emotions get the better of us. I've been there myself; a life's work starts to feel threatened, your savings are on the line, and you've got bills to pay at home. The fear kicks in. That fear is absolutely real and totally understandable.

I have a wise and talented client and mentor, Dr. Randy Lais, who I've worked with for many years. He sometimes lectures about Maslow's hierarchy as it relates to business. A concept familiar to researchers in psychology and the social sciences, Maslow's hierarchy is a pyramid that explains in which order we must attend to our various needs in order to reach the top of the pyramid—which is self-actualization, a high-level concept where we've arrived at our best and most true self, only possible when we've tended to our baser needs (such as the need for food, water, and sleep.)

SELF-ACTUALIZATION
morality, creativity, spontaneity, acceptance, experience, purpose, meaning and inner potential

SELF-ESTEEM
confidence, achievement, respect of others, the need to be a unique individual

LOVE AND BELONGING
friendship, family, intimacy, sense of connection

SAFETY AND SECURITY
health, employment, property, family and social abilty

PHYSIOLOGICAL NEEDS
breathing, food, water, shelter, clothing, sleep

Dr. Lais talks about how business owners fall victim to *reacting* based on either a perceived or real lack of security—like with Maslow's hierarchy, when we are reactive and letting fear rule our actions, we're making decisions that are what I call crisis-focused, or attributable to the survivor mentality. These served our ancestors just fine when we were out in the caves looking for a safe place to lie down for the night with our families—one where we wouldn't be eaten by any lions or bears—but making decisions out of emotion and fear doesn't make for the best business policy when it comes to successfully reaching our objectives. When we do that, we tend to overcorrect, give up too early, make hasty judgments, and indulge in other problematic (albeit, again, completely understandable) behavior.

So this is where marketing decisions and marriage come to an amicable split (pun maybe a little bit intended). In order to keep yourself from making emotional decisions when it comes to marketing, you need to put up safety measures. (Remember those rubber bowling bumpers that keep your ball in the lane?). Those safety measures come in the form of strategic thinking.

What We Talk About When We Talk About Strategy

For me, strategy is all about taking the long view. It's being able to get past that feeling of being in the trenches (where a lot of fear, darkness and, reactive stuff lives) and see things from a better point of view, where you can watch everything play out and react accordingly (without the resulting emotional decisions that come out of panic and trenches-thought). And it's particularly important to think about strategy *before* you get too deep into any project, especially because, like me, you've probably got a lot of things going on, and you want to make sure that you get the most out of your marketing budget.

I'm totally with you on that, and that's why I advocate for strategy. Like a football coach who is watching a game tape, a strategic vantage point allows you to see all possibilities and have a plan to execute in all of those possibilities. This isn't to say that things won't come at you from time to time (sacks from a blind spot, if we're going to continue the football metaphor), but that for the most part, if you've positioned your players correctly and you've got your plan for the play-by-play down, there won't be so many surprises. And when there *are* surprises, if you have a strategy in place, you'll be able to continue making first downs, even if you're slowed up a bit. Because when you play with strategy, you play with confidence.

How Emotion Gets in Your Way (and How You Can Rise Above)

Emotions can often get the better of decision makers before, during, and after campaigns. When these emotions take hold, the options start to seem a little murky, and those who would normally think of themselves as level-headed are anything but. You may have experienced this in your own work; perhaps you've felt "burned" by a particular medium before. You may have spent a great deal of money on a television ad that landed flat. Or you may have preconceived ideas of how effective a certain medium will be for your target market. Or you may be in the midst of what could be a great campaign in the end, but your fear causes you to act prematurely and pull the plug before you've gotten traction.

Whenever you can identify your emotional triggers and understand the reactions you're having (ask yourself: is this rational, or is this emotional?), you make it easier to *overcome* those emotions. I advise my clients to counteract emotions by relying on data—looking at analytics and facts rather than letting a "gut feeling" rule the day. And if you look at the overall data for each advertisement venue as a whole *in addition to* the data you've tracked for similar products, market segments, and times, you have a good chance of anticipating where these so-called slow-burning campaigns might fall. For instance, I've found that the first weeks of radio and television campaigns are sometimes slow to gain traction when you're in the midst of awareness building. Early returns might convince an emotional person to pull the plug on this effort. A rational person would look at the data for how long it takes a brand to build awareness and see that they needed more time. In the alternative, making adjustments is a better bet to help you stay out of your own way, rather than cutting a campaign entirely short. All of this is part of PETMAG, a handy helper I developed for rising above emotions and making strategic decisions to get successful results.

What Is PETMAG?

PETMAG is a handy acronym I like to use to help remember the system for executing non-emotional marketing decisions. The first step is to create a **plan,** the importance of which was detailed in Chapter 5. Without a plan, you simply won't know where you're going, and you're setting yourself up to have your emotions and temporary momentum (be it upward or downward)—not your strategy—be your guide. Having a plan means that you've taken the guesswork out of the marketing that you intend to do, and

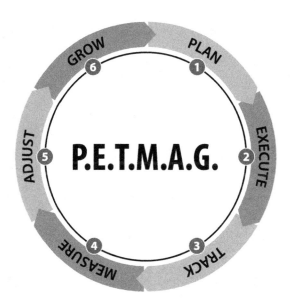

the fewer cracks in your foundation created by guesswork and gut reactions, the fewer places emotion has to leak in. The second step is all about **execution**—the all-important follow through. By designating a point person for each objective and ruthlessly following through on each and every campaign and initiative you have in your plan, you start to see that progress; the ball gets farther and farther down the field.

Tracking and measuring are crucial in your quest to keep emotion out of the equation; without tracking and measuring, you won't have any data to rely on. Luckily for all of us, today's world is full of analytic tools—some of them even free—that can help us collect, understand, and act on data. Google Analytics, Facebook Analytics, third-party aggregators like Klout and Hootsuite, are all tools that can help you analyze data in real time for campaigns. You can make use of targeted links (www.yourcompany.com/radio is a simple example of how you might track referrals from a radio ad as they become web conversions), hashtags that coincide with promotions, microsite landing pages, and more to gather specific information about how traffic is being driven to your doors (literal or figurative doors; the same thing applies to brick and mortar as much as it applies to an online presence). And no matter what promotions you've got going on, you should *always* be asking every customer you interact with how they found out about you. This can help you get a handle on otherwise nebulous word-of-mouth trends as well as test out specific advertising venues (Facebook ad, direct mail, other).

Next, there's reacting to your data (*not* your emotions)—if you need to **adjust**, don't be afraid to do so. You may find that your campaign isn't reaching your target with laser precision, or that the type of messaging assigned to your target isn't in alignment with your goal for that campaign. Watching data collected from a full complement of tracking tools is how you learn what's working, what's almost working, and what's not quite working. But a word of caution: like your retirement portfolio and the stock market, it's something you should follow closely, but not *too* closely—make sure to allow time for trends to develop. Watching a portfolio take a nosedive in a downturn incites fear in the hearts of even the most well-heeled investor, making them amp up their losses while, ironically, attempting to cut them by pulling out early. Just as good investors know that for every bear, there's a bull around the corner, and that market timing is not something you should try at home, good marketers know that you have to apply ample patience when looking at and adjusting according to data.

Finally, and most wonderfully, you've got an imperative: to **grow**. If you follow the steps outlined in PETMAG, growth is the natural result. Taking the guesswork out allows you to experience wonderful returns with fewer of the headaches. After you've made your plan, this is where the fun can begin: you know who your customer is, you know who your competitor is, and you know your brand inside and out. You believe in your brand; you know that what *you* offer is unique, and now you get to see your leads blossom into customers and your customers bulk up your bottom line. I can think of a new-in-town restaurant I worked with on a geo-targeted, age-specific Facebook campaign that saw a 1,000% growth in two weeks just from that one ad. When we heard those results, it was hard to stop another major emotion from cropping up: joy! And *that's* an emotion I can definitely get down with.

Going back to the football field for a moment, I want you to consider how games are played (and more important, how they are won). Often, they aren't won in giant sweeping gestures—the Hail Mary pass that lands true to its target, or the QB who scrambles out of an attempted sack only to run the ball the length of the field for the game-winning touchdown. Instead, games are won in small plays, and small increments. Sometimes it takes a team two or three plays to get that next first down; moving four yards at a time doesn't call for calling it quits. Sometimes it's going to take you a bit to get your momentum going, too. Instead of giving up at the first sign of trouble, your strategy should be based on a deep understanding of how to keep moving forward even when the going gets tough. By relying on strategy rather than on your emotions, executing and adjusting as you go along, I have faith that you'll get there.

Case Study: A Monument to Marketing

When done right and acted upon strategically, tracking our referrals and segmenting our data can be tremendously helpful in guiding new marketing strategy (or adjustments to existing marketing strategy). When comparing the data from a Facebook campaign, an SEO campaign, and a direct mail campaign to see how each was (or was not) increasing inquiries for one business, for example, I could understand who was converting and at what dollar value. I was able to put a factual, rather than emotional, value on that data and allow it to reveal a pattern. And the importance of tracking and its ability to reveal patterns and useful information cannot be overstated; if you're not bothering to track your marketing and turn that tracking into data, you might as well be throwing your money away. And while love is blind, data is not; it won't deceive you, it won't change unless you do something to massage it, and it doesn't come to you with any baggage—it just is what it is. Recognizing the value of data and tracking worked particularly well for another client I work with when it came to one of the oldest tricks in the book—physical signage. I was skeptical when this owner of a medical practice said that he thought a monument-style sign outside his office could drive in more referral traffic than anything else he was doing. But then he showed me the data to back it up: he and his employees had polled his incoming customers and the sign outperformed every other avenue; it was the number-one referral over radio and television.

I learned a couple lessons from this. One was that had I not seen that report, I might have let my gut feeling lead me to overspend in areas that were just plain ineffective, shorting the idea of a sign just because I had a *feeling* that other advertising avenues would perform better. Another was that digital analytics are not *all* you need to rely upon when it comes to assessing your marketing strategy. I come from a background of wasting not and wanting not, learning to use each part of a chicken dinner, down to the bones and skin to make stock (that tip is courtesy of my mother, I admit). Small and startup businesses need to make use of every asset at their disposal; in this case, the client was training *every one of his employees at every touch point* to ask customers how they found out about the business. That's where his data was coming from, and it spoke loud and clear.

Having a clear plan of attack for making decisions will help you stay away from making emotional choices when logic tells you to act differently, but having a clear plan of attack means staying current on trends, tools and techniques. I'm here to help.

Visit: www.DontBuyADuck.com/bonus or text DUCK to 58885.

CHAPTER TEN

The Smartest Way to Set a Marketing Budget

Budgeting isn't everyone's favorite task, that's for sure (well, maybe accountants and financial planner types—but there's a reason you and I are marketers first, right?). But at this moment, I can't think of a more important task to talk about. Because here's the thing about budgeting for marketing: it's a non-negotiable. And I know you're busy, and I know you've got people on your payroll or other departments full of people who deal with the numbers, but my best, biggest, imagine it underlined-bolded-all-capped piece of advice to you is that you *must set your marketing budget.*

Speaking of the financial planner types, they like to talk about paying yourself first when it comes to setting a household budget. And what they're talking about is socking money away in your savings before you start spending it on anything else, whether it's necessities or extras. This is essentially investing in yourself; it's making sure you prioritize your future financial security by creating a line item that goes straight to your savings.

Even though it's on the expense side, setting a marketing budget is no different. If you're a business owner, it's all about investing in yourself—your vision. If you're in charge of setting a marketing budget, it's investing in the company you work for, in all of the hard work you and your team do to make your product or service really shine.

Personally, I'm a business owner. I've sacrificed time with my family, the security of depending on someone else for a paycheck, the calm walk through an already well-trodden path. But I've done it because I had a vision. If you started your own business, *you're* doing it because *you* have a vision. If you're in charge of marketing for a larger company, you presumably believe in that product, and that vision. Why wouldn't you want to share that vision with the world? If you're doing what you're doing to make your customers happy, to solve a problem, to provide a service, you should *absolutely* want to invest in marketing that service (or product) and letting your future patrons know you're there for them.

If you've come this far and done this many steps—making an in-depth plan, defining yourself as a brand, developing a dynamite product—setting a marketing budget is simply the next rational step to take. Just as you would budget for your mortgage or rent on your office, for your lease on your company vehicles and equipment, for your employee overhead—marketing is a necessary expense that you have to budget for. It's not elective or an extra. It's not frivolous. And by setting a line item in your budget for marketing, you're ensuring that there's no room to make it expendable. We're all incredibly busy, and many of us are spread remarkably thin, even as our businesses are soaring well into the black. All the more reason to set a marketing budget that you can anticipate, one that ensures you stay in that successful place—and stay top of mind.

I can't emphasize this point enough—even in times of relative success, the marketing budget should not be looked at as a surplus. If you want to earmark some of your increased earnings for R&D, or expansion, or any other venture, that's fine. But never let any of those things eat away at your marketing budget. Like a CD or a portfolio of options that needs vesting, think of that money as untouchable—without a hefty fee.

So the first step with budgeting, as with so many of the goals I advocate in this book, is to just get started. This is all part of calling those plays and moving down the field. It's far too easy to get paralyzed, to naysay the value of marketing—if you're busy, if you're unsure of the ROI, if marketing feels like a mystery to you. But this is why I've so strongly argued for bulking up your practices around data and tracking. No longer a mystery, no longer shrouded in the murkiness of doubt, marketing has real values attached to it, real costs and real dividends. Armed with your plan and your data, you can make adjustments as you go along, rather than blindly slashing and burning something when you have a "gut feeling" that it's not working. You can, with undeniable precision, remove a piece of advertising that's not working and move that money over to another advertising medium that might do better based on what the data is telling you. You can hold your marketing dollars, your partners, and your contracts accountable. And you can keep moving the ball down the field.

My Method for Marketing Success

Over the years, I've developed my own method for setting a marketing budget. It's important to note that it's a *method* rather than a formula—while I've suggested certain amounts here, they are certainly by no means meant to fit every business. Depending on your sector, size, location, and a host of other variable factors, you might find that these numbers will need some adjustment. And those adjustments should be relatively easy to make, especially since at this point you've got a plan and the data to back it up! (Right? Good!)

There's another consideration to make before you begin to use this budgeting method for marketing. You still need to make sure that your profit margins are healthy. This is the equivalent of making sure you have a strong foundation before you start to build a house. You want to build the best possible house you can build, one where you can really grow and thrive. To keep that house safe, you need that strong foundation.

According to a great article from Caron Beesley at the U.S. Small Business Administration's (SBA) blog,[1] the "safe" profit margin range starts at 10%, and I couldn't agree more —although I would like to see it much higher than 10%. If you have margins lower than that, it's a little too soon to be talking about a marketing budget. Remember: even if you're running a small business, you have to understand your stability based on what's proportional for you—you can't be skating by on 7% margins and think that's fine just because you don't bring in that much gross revenue anyway!

---

[1] http://www.sba.gov/blogs/how-set-marketing-budget-fits-your-business-goals-and-provides-high-return-investment

Bearing that in mind, I've broken down a few options for setting a marketing budget, categorized by risk, as a percentage of gross sales revenue. They are:

Marketing Budget			
% of sale revenue			
1	2 to 3%	=	Very safe
2	5 to 6%	=	Bolder
3	8 to 12%	=	Aggressive
4	> 13%	=	Risky

The SBA's statistics, though slightly more conservative (I'm more bullish on marketing; I'm a marketer!) nicely dovetail these; that same article says: "As a general rule, small businesses with revenues less than $5 million should allocate 7–8 percent of their revenues to marketing. This budget should be split between 1) brand development costs...and 2) the costs of promoting your business (campaigns, advertising, events, etc.)."

I didn't have an aha moment that led me to come up with this method—that's part of why I don't call it a formula, it's not written in stone. And I'm happy to find that the SBA, a reliable resource for any strategic businessperson, independently arrived at figures that support my method. But on the other hand, I'm not surprised; this method came from years of analyzing and averaging *data*.

Analyzing Risk:
What Might Be Right for You

Some people are risk seeking, while others might be more inclined to sit back and watch what happens. This is true of life (is your idea of a relaxing vacation skiing down a black diamond, or is it sitting by the pool?), the stock market (do you bet big, or go for slow gains over time?), and more. The type of risk I'm talking about here shouldn't necessarily be driven by those psychological impulses, though (remember: you want to act on *data*, not *emotions*). Instead, take into account what stage your business is in. Are you just stepping into the market, looking to make a splash and ramp up growth? Are you in a space with little to no competition? Are you richer in resources, or are you more of a Little Engine That Could? There's a budget to fit each industry, each business, and every goal. And just a general note: if you're a new business, it should be said that you'll probably be spending in the higher echelons in the beginning, when you're trying to gain market awareness and penetration. You can scale back or forward from there as you see fit.

2 to 3% = Very Safe

Little Engine types, this might work for you: definitely in the short term, and maybe even in the long, depending on your situation. If you're a startup company, or just newer to marketing, you might want to be cautious upon entry, putting only 2 to 3% of your top-line revenue toward a marketing budget. You might not be able to risk more of your resources at this point, and that's absolutely fine: the important thing is just to start. Remember, as your revenue grows, your marketing dollars can grow, too.

Something else to consider: if you're not in the position to spend much money on advertising, you need to get creative with PR, partnerships, and grassroots efforts to make up for some of the monetary slack. Cultivating brand ambassadors both internally and externally, getting some traction when it comes to press clips, goodwill, and cross-promotional opportunities—all of this provides returns that sometimes will far exceed what money can buy. When I was starting out in music, I learned that sometimes there was nothing better than getting out there face to face with the fans and relying on grassroots methods to gain exposure. I wholeheartedly identify with this level of marketing spending, and I think that even 2 to 3%, while it might not seem like that much, can absolutely make a difference.

5 to 6% = Bolder

At this point, you're ratcheting up the stakes a little bit. Maybe you started at the bottom tier, saw the results you needed, and put more resources behind your marketing. Maybe your core product launch was successful, and you've got more brand recognition to lend heft to your efforts. Or maybe you're a business that has gained some recognition locally, expanded your budget accordingly, and you're trying to break into some new niches of your market. But one thing is clear: at this point, you're recognizing that your marketing spending is an investment, and just as you would with any investment, you're embracing the gains.

When you start getting into this category of marketing spending, you're able to reach for some of the higher-hanging fruit. While working at the 2–3% level, you got some experience with word-of-mouth, with street teams, with good press, and with social. You took your DIY ethos and made it work, spending thriftily but still spending, still gaining market share. Now is not the time to leave those hard-won lessons behind, but rather to begin to scale. If you're advertising on the radio, it might be time to move into those higher-priced, drive-time spots. If you're buying TV ads, start looking to increase the frequency in an effort to drive awareness.

Annual Gross Sales Revenue: $3,000,000		
Itemized:	$	%
Salary/Labor	$ 600,000	20%
Lease/Mortgage	$ 90,000	3%
Utilities	$ 30,000	1%
Marketing/Advertising	$ 150,000	5%
Office Equipment	$ 90,000	3%
	$ 300,000	1
	$ 30,000	

Annual Marketing Budget: $150,000	Amount of Budget to Dedicate
Digital (online) ads	$ 12,000
Direct mail campaign	$ 6,000
Social media ads	$ 12,000
Billboards	$ 22,000
Network TV	$ 24,000
Cable TV	$ 18,000
Print	$ 12,000
Radio	$ 24,000
E-blasts	$ 2,500
PR	$ 3,000
Blogs/E-newsletters	$ 2,500
Sales materials	$ 6,000
Trade shows	$ 6,000

8 to 12% = Aggressive

This is the sweet spot: growth mode. You are comfortable in your standing. All of your hard work and frequency of messages have paid off, and you are a household name in your market. You might have built up a sizable war chest at this point—connections are there, partnerships are coming easier, and you have an undeniable core customer base. You want to reach new customers, too, so you're spending more to get even more market share. If this is the case, it makes sense to be aggressive. There's more at stake, too—you're taking a bigger slice of the pie to spend on your marketing budget. But you wouldn't have gotten to this point if you didn't have a great product to give. You wouldn't be talking to this many people still if you didn't have a genuine audience for your product or service.

There's also another point to this level of marketing, one underscored by necessity. This is part of what I mean when I say that the specific industry you're in heavily dictates your marketing spending, too—if you're in a business that doesn't have many perishables, there's not necessarily a time sensitivity to what you're working with. If, on the other hand, you're a farm-to-table restaurant in a competitive market and you've just bought a bunch of heirloom perishables for your opening weekend, you're going to need to market, and market hard. If you're doing a slower ramp-up, you have a little more wiggle room. But sometimes, you're going to need to *start* with this level of spending, rather than working up to it. And if that's not a risk you're willing or able to take, it might be time to rethink the plan a little bit.

> 13% = Risky

There's no way around it: spending 13% of your gross sales revenue is a risk. I say this without judgment or ulterior motive—remember, totally without emotion, we're letting the numbers speak for themselves! (Again, I want to mention that in the early days of your business, when you're establishing yourself, a greater portion of dollars and time may go toward building that awareness.)

Some companies might need to immediately spend in this strata because of what they're selling, where they're selling it, or how their business is structured. But others have the ability to be at this level because they have a proven track record, not just with their products but with their marketing, too. They have the data to support allotting this kind of cash to marketing—they have the buy-in of the C-suite, and they have it for a reason. Other than stability, another upside to being financially able to take this sort of risk is that quite frankly, things get more *fun* when you're at this point. You can start to think blue sky with your messaging and campaigns. You can try new things. My point of view is not so much that you should take risks just because you want to, but rather that you have the financial cushioning to do so, and you're strategically following up on various leads and options.

Of course, just as with the restaurant example I gave in the previous spending strata, there are businesses that need to jump into crowded marketplaces and quickly gain share. But no matter the motivation, the math has to line up, the data has to be there, and the *plan* has to be in place. As I've talked about throughout the book, no one—not industry giants like Coca-Cola or Starbucks, not once-spritely startups like Uber or Airbnb—*no one* can expect to effectively market without a plan. And these figures, even at the riskier echelons, are protective measures. Like a moat around a castle, the line item makes marketing a priority and keeps it there.

Planning also provides something priceless: peace of mind. When you approach marketing spending like an investment, rather than a luxury item, your psychological state can reflect that. If you believe in yourself and you believe in your product, you owe it to yourself to invest in your own success. But what's more, *you owe it to your customer.* You owe them the benefit of learning all that you have to offer. You owe them an option that will make their lives better, whether it's by starting the day off with a truly amazing cup of coffee or going to sleep knowing that the patented technology in your home alarm system is keeping their family safe.

What you *do*, no matter *what* you do, is change lives. Why would you want to keep that quiet? You have a great product, but your target customer can never say "yes" to you if they don't know about you. You owe it to yourself to get your product in front of those customers so that they get the chance to say "YES!"

Times change, marketing platforms change, who knows what each new day brings. As marketers it's our job to keep up with the most accurate and most recent marketing information. Visit our site: www.DontBuyADuck.com/bonus or text DUCK to 58885 to access special bonuses that will provide great value to you and your business.

CHAPTER ELEVEN

The End Zone

Now that we've reached the end of our journey together, I feel like I can finally reveal the secret of marketing success to you. You've earned it.

Okay. Are you ready?

The secret is…there is no secret. There are no silver bullet solutions here, no set-it-and-forget-it stuff. What we—marketers, that is—do, isn't sexy, despite what our fictional advertising colleagues on AMC might have led the layperson to believe. Don Draper we're not. It's not about looks and pomade. It's a lot of legwork, a lot of heavy lifting, and a lot of day-in-and-day-out grind. Just like our gridiron heroes, marketing is a mission on which we must shed blood, sweat, and tears. But, also like football, it's entirely a meritocracy: anyone can get to the end zone if they work hard and smart enough. If they keep making first downs. If they keep getting that ball down the field, a yard at a time. Real work practically *guarantees* real progress (as much as anything can ever be guaranteed—but that's another book entirely).

In my 15 years in the industry—and in my lifetime as a student of marketing, reaching all the way back to when I was a kid playing in my first band and sending out my own press kits via bulk mail—I've been fortunate to learn a lot of lessons. I've failed on more than one occasion, but I've also seen success. I've learned from some of the best people: my colleagues and my clients. But my first important marketing lessons, I learned from Quackers.

As bad as I feel about spending my allowance on Quackers, taking him from the farm and bringing him along in that station wagon, eventually finding a more peaceful home for him in a neighbor's pond, I'm forever indebted to the lesson I learned from him, because everything stems from that lesson. Because of Quackers and that valuable allowance I lost in one shot, I learned to look before I leapt. I learned not to gamble on unknown entities, no matter the context. I learned the value of a plan, the proper tools, and proper organization. I learned the importance of exhaustive research and nurturing a natural curiosity. I learned that if you don't execute, all of your tools can easily be for naught. I learned if you don't make adjustments (like pulling over the car and letting a giant, confused, and probably justifiably angry bird out of the car and into the pond) as you go along, you'll only get further stuck in situations better left in the past. And I learned that while emotion may rule our hearts, it doesn't have to rule the day, at least not when it comes to marketing that works.

I'm so honored that you've taken this journey with me down the field and into the end zone. Along with my team at The Artist Evolution (www.theartistevolution.com), I'm always happy to talk marketing—whether it's coming up with a plan for a startup business to make a splash or for a cornerstone entity to branch out and reach new customers. I'm certainly not the only resource out there for this; you might have more than enough to say on the matter after you've implemented the tools in this book into your own marketing practice! But I'm happy to continue to be a resource where and when I can, especially if I can save even one person from going through the dubious experience of taking home an ungainly farm animal. You can also join my email list by contacting me at info@derekchampagne.com—once you're on that list, you'll receive key insights from successful business owners, consultants, and marketing decision makers who I interview each month in an effort to collect and share more marketing knowledge with the world at large.

Whether or not you and I cross paths again, I hope that you're spared the knowledge of what it feels like to be pummeled by feathers. But more than that? I wish you all the success in the world. You've got the vision, after all. Now start letting people know about it.

This might be the last chapter of the book, but it's not the end of receiving useful tools, techniques, and cutting edge marketing ideas. If you haven't already, be sure to visit: www.DontBuyADuck. com/bonus or text DUCK to 58885 to register this book and receive special bonuses available only to readers.

CPSIA information can be obtained
at www.ICGtesting.com
Printed in the USA
FSOW04n0511070317
31524FS